# Lost Architecture of the Rio Grande Borderlands

Number 7:

FRONTERAS SERIES, sponsored by

Texas A&M International University

José Roberto Juárez, General Editor

W. Eugene George

# Lost Architecture

## OF THE RIO GRANDE BORDERLANDS

*Foreword by* Ricardo Paz Treviño

*Color Photographs by* W. Eugene George

TEXAS A&M UNIVERSITY PRESS College Station

Library of Congress Cataloging-in-Publication Data

George, Eugene.

    Lost architecture of the Rio Grande borderlands / W. Eugene

George ;foreword by Ricardo Paz Treviño ; color photographs by

W. Eugene George. — 1st ed.

      p. cm.—(Fronteras series ; no. 7)

    Includes bibliographical references and index.

    ISBN-13: 978-1-60344-011-0 (cloth : alk. paper)

    ISBN-10: 1-60344-011-9 (cloth : alk. paper)

    1. Falcon Reservoir Region (Mexico and Tex.)—Antiquities.

2. Historic buildings—Falcon Reservoir Region (Mexico and Tex.)

3. Architecture—Falcon Reservoir Region (Mexico and Tex.)

4. Texas—Antiquities 5. Salvage archaeology—Falcon Reservoir

Region (Mexico and Tex.) I. Title.

F392.R5G47 2008

976.4'483—dc22

                                2007039361

FRONTISPIECE: La Iglesia de Nuestra Señora del Refugio—Our Lady
of Refuge—Guerrero Viejo, Tamaulipas, Mexico. Photograph by the
author, August 1983.

# Contents

# Illustrations

Documentation of the various projects related to the Falcón Reservoir—offshoots of the River Basin Survey and Salvage Project—are deposited in the Texas Archaeological Research Laboratory (TARL), the University of Texas at Austin. Permission has been granted for publication of all photographs from the TARL collections. Considering the circumstances under which the material was collected and the neglect it suffered for many years, that it survives at all is little short of a miracle. Thanks are due Carolyn Spock, TARL, who conducted invaluable archival research on the work of the salvage archaeologists of the 1950s.

Illustration 25: Until 1850, locally produced split cypress shakes were used for structures in the Escandón settlements that had shingle roofs. Evidence in the photograph of the house at San Bartolo indicated that the original roof had been replaced after 1850. By the mid-nineteenth century, sawn white cedar shingles, produced in Michigan, were transported down the Mississippi to New Orleans, then transshipped by steamboat up the Rio Grande to Roma for distribution throughout the territory. The spacing of the nailing strips and the technique employed in the application of the shingles in the San Bartolo dwelling indicate that these shingles would, historically, have been sawn white cedar from Michigan. The joist sizes were also more appropriate for American-influenced roof construction.

Illustrations 38–40: James Bryan Boyd, a police officer and avocational archaeologist, has worked for many years in the borderlands area of Texas. He has photographed numerous sites around the Falcón Reservoir.

Illustration 41: Villa de Señor San Ignacio de Loyola de Revilla was founded on October 10, 1750, on Rancho Los Moros in the present state of Tamaulipas, Mexico. The site was moved three times before it was situated in its present location in a bend of the Rio Salado. The name was changed to Guerrero in 1827 following the revolt against Spain. The plan of Revilla was accessed by the author at the Archivo General de Indias in Seville on January 5, 1984.

Illustration 50: Nuestra Señora del Refugio, the second church on the site, was built with stones from the first church and stands beside the ruins of the church's tower. Built of red sandstone called las Piedras de la Virgen, the stones were quarried from two hills southeast of the town. According to Lori Brown McVey this site was used solely as a quarry for the church. The quarry is some distance west of the present banks of the Rio Salado, but there are indications that the river may have once run closer to the quarry. The stones, weighing 150 to 300 pounds, may have been rafted downstream to the town.

When I was asked to write the foreword for *Lost Architecture of the Rio Grande Border-lands,* I accepted the challenge to revisit memories of my childhood with mixed emotions. As a direct descendant of the original Treviños who first settled in this area—on my mother's maternal and paternal side, as was sometimes done in those days—my memories are bittersweet. They center primarily on the town of Revilla on the Mexican side of the Rio Grande—founded in the 1750s and later renamed Guerrero Viejo. It was one of several towns, villages, and ranches whose inhabitants and livestock were displaced when a U.S./Mexico Joint Task Force called for the development of a controlled-level reservoir by the damming of the Rio Grande River (or the Río Bravo del Norte as it is called in Mexico). Pleas from locals who opposed the project because of adverse social effects fell on deaf ears. The dam was constructed—its white concrete ramparts stark against the blue Texas/Mexican sky—at once creating a much-needed water source, but effectively wiping Revilla/Guerrero Viejo from the face of the earth (as well as many more humble sites on the Texas side of the river). Falcón, the name chosen for the dam and the reservoir was both appropriate—a bicultural word for an indigenous bird—and ironic—this ferocious bird of prey along with most of its habitat was obliterated. All in the name of progress. And like the *falcón,* the inhabitants of Guerrero Viejo disappeared from the landscape. They were forcibly relocated to Guerrero Nuevo—a government-sponsored settlement totally devoid of personality, character, and, most tragically, history. From this elevated vantage point, these displaced souls watched as a body of water larger than the combined area of nearby Laredo and Nuevo Laredo enveloped the parched valleys and canyons that had been their home for generations. Just as surely as the water crept up the sides of homes, church, school, and shops, just as certainly as the few possessions left behind floated away and were swept down the Rio Grande's winding course to the Gulf of Mexico, the soul of Revilla/Guerrero Viejo was relegated to the memories of those who had known it. And just as the church's arch was a visible testimony to the sunken town of Revilla/Guerrero Viejo, the faith and love of the people of Revilla/Guerrero Viejo rose above the hardship to build new towns, new lives, and a new future. My paternal and maternal grandparents were born and raised in Revilla/Guerrero Viejo, and all my great-grandparents, the entire "Treviñada," were buried there. I was part of the new life that sprang from this forced evacuation of my ancestors, and I consider myself, my extended family, and my offspring the embodiment of their hope for the future.

Undoubtedly, my most vivid memories focus on El Día de Los Muertos. Every year on November 2, as well as anniversary dates of loved ones, various members of the families would come back to their beloved, sunken town. Not all the inhabitants of Revilla/Guerrero Viejo had left when the water came. In the church's cemetery behind the appropriately named Nuestra Señora Del Refugio (Our Lady of Refuge) lay the graves of many Treviño family members, the early settlers: those that could not and did not leave. So we came to them on those special days, and for us children the mournful cries of our elders cast only a slight pall over the impending boat ride to the protruding church's arch. On both sides of the reservoir's shores, there was an almost carnival-like atmosphere with vendors hawking bunches of flowers ("*F-l-o-r-e-s- para los muertos! F-l-o-r-e-s para los muertos!*"), fruits, candles, and other religious objects that we would offer to the dead. Small boats for hire dotted the shorelines ready for families who then motored to the only visible remnant of the town, the stone arches of the church. It seemed that it was always dusk when the ceremonies began. This was a matter of practicality as people worked a full day before coming to the shorelines with their families. And often the overland trip had taken many hours as they came from various places in the United States and Mexico.

I also remember the cold or sometimes the heat. Much like the land itself, the weather was an exercise in extremes. Bitterly cold in some years, oppressively hot in others. There was, however, one commonality: the wind. The sharp wind swept across the nearly flat landscape and the mirrorlike surface of the reservoir, carrying the mournful cries of the old ladies dressed in black. Always the crying. Sometimes it was difficult to determine exactly where the crying was coming from—the ladies, the wind, or perhaps the murky water itself. Just as surely as the wind reddened my cheeks, chapped my lips, and burned my eyes when I turned into it, I knew that same wind could carry voices from the past—my ancestors literally reaching out and speaking to me. I would often try to hide my face from the wind by peering into the dark water, imagining the town submerged below me.

The small boats we rode in always seemed to be surrounded by floating debris. Always. One would think these remnants of the town would eventually float away, but they were always there. A haunting reminder that those whose graves we came to honor and remember, and whom I had only known in the abstract, had actually lived and breathed and eaten and worked directly below the flotilla of overburdened boats. Getting to the town from the shore was not a quick or easy trip; it was not unusual to spend several hours making the pilgrimage. And since the reservoir lay on the U.S.-Mexico border, our relatives from the Mexican side would often meet us at the ruin. What a bizarre, watery family reunion—its attendants struggling to stay balanced in their boats while greeting relatives, separated by the waters of the Falcón Reservoir.

The pinnacle of the facade of Our Lady of Refuge was a single eight-foot stone and stucco arch. It rose out of the water like a ghostly doorway, beckoning its visitors. This was our destination. Overfilled and running low in the water, the boats carried the mourners and their offerings. Some families hired readily available priests and nuns to accompany them on the journey to the site. Once there, prayers were offered for the dead, the town, and the living. What a surreal and exciting scene for a child to watch from a small bobbing boat. Amid the wails and prayers, I recall looking up at the stark white archway, its curved stones defiantly standing against the lapping water. The high point for the children was to actually make the offerings. What child doesn't enjoy throwing things into the water? As the items in our boat were blessed and presented, I would drop them reverently into the thick, dark water. The area surrounding the boats quickly became littered with fruit, flowers, and pieces of *pan de muerto*. But what stood out most profoundly, both in my memory and on the dark water itself, were the yellow buds of the *zempasuchil*. These colorful marigolds appeared to dance on the water—a mocking reminder that regardless of the ruins entombed below, life on the surface continues.

We always loved visiting the area surrounding the reservoir and one of its neighboring towns, San Ignacio, Texas, where several members of both my maternal and paternal family had settled. In these remote ranching areas—Los Ojuelos, Mirando, Randado, Cuevitas, Roma, Las Escobas, Los Saénz, El Sauz, San Roman, many without running water and electricity, not to mention television—it was not uncommon for families to sit outside on the porch at night and listen as the old folks regaled their listeners with stories of treasures buried for safe-keeping from the frequent attacks by bandidos and Indians in the area.

I grew up hearing stories of intermittent Indian attacks on remote, unprotected settlements that occurred as recently as the late 1800s. Even today, a seemingly inexhaustible supply of flint arrowheads litters the terrain. One has only to shuffle through the dry earth to reveal similar arrowheads possibly meant for my ancestors. In response to this lethal threat, many of the surrounding ranching communities developed creative methods of constructing secure, fortified houses with locally available materials. The Treviño fortified house in San Ignacio, Texas, one of many built throughout the area, still stands as a prime example of a secure home built to outlast the hostility and ensure the legacy of my family's homestead. Unfortunately, only a handful of these fortified houses survive, proud monuments to lives carved out of the harsh, unforgiving land.

During my teen years, probable descendents of those same marauding Indians once again entered our lives. An integral part of their religious and spiritual rituals calls for a transcendent communication with their deceased ancestors. To facilitate this experience, the Indians require peyote, a spineless, dome-shaped cactus that grows abundantly in area ranches. Every February, members of the Indian tribes that originally inhabited these areas would travel from their reservations in Oklahoma, New Mexico, and Arizona to Laredo, Texas, to participate in the annual George Washington's birthday celebration and parade. (The celebration was started by the Improved Order of the Red Men, local chapter Yaqui Tribe No. 59, whose members included prominent locals of both Mexican and American ancestry.) Many of these Native Americans would ride in the parade on their pinto ponies wearing full ceremonial regalia, including war paint, feather headdresses, tomahawks, knives, and bows and arrows. After the parade, many of the Indians, including their chieftains, shamans (medicine men), and warriors would drive back to Los Ojuelos (the magical natural springs), the ranch where my paternal grandfather was the *caporal* (foreman) to procure from us and our neighbors the peyote buttons used for generations in their religious and sacrificial ceremonies.

What was an enterprising teen to do? Sell peyote buttons to them, of course! On many weekends, we would collect the wild peyote cacti, trim and sun-dry them on large homemade wooden platforms, and package the dried peyote buttons by the thousands in small burlap sacks. Immediately upon their arrival at the Los Ojuelos ranch, the Indian chiefs would proclaim the going price for the peyote buttons that year, and we and many of our neighbors would be paid in crisp one-hundred dollar bills—equivalent to four dollars for every one-thousand buttons. Afterward, the tribe would head off to initiate their annual religious ceremony. Under the darkest night sky, we would crawl under their parked trucks and horse trailers and stealthily watch in awe as their sacramental ceremony began. The heat from their massive bonfires warmed my face while the smoke stung my ever-widening eyes at the scene that unfolded before us. The Indians, falling into a hallucinatory trance would dance and scream and sing and yell until the sun rose. These ceremonies would sometimes last for several days—nonstop.

Incredible, vivid memories. Shared experiences. I recall these moments in my life with fondness and reverence for the past. For many natives of the Rio Grande Valley like myself, our family histories are made up of such stories. They are preserved in the retelling. Having heard these stories, viewed yellowing pictures, and seen in the eyes of my elders the vibrant life that came before ours, I know that we are truly blessed. Some families have seen their members scattered by strife and time—their legacy relegated to epitaphs—like many inhabitants of the towns and ranches that simply died out slowly, or in the case of Revilla and its sister settlements—a fast and violent underwater demise.

So where does this leave me and my family? The other descendants of Guerrero Viejo? The children of determined settlers who built fortified houses? We have been burdened with the grave and wonderful responsibility of making our past a living history. Much like the multicolored, multitextured quilts lovingly sewn by the *abuelas* as they watched the children play, the memories, writings, pictures, songs, and campfire stories make up the very fabric of our family. By themselves, each square represents only a snapshot. But when woven together, when bound with love and secured with pride, these individual pieces become a map of our history, of our family. The Treviños.

—Ricardo Paz-Treviño

The Hispanic ranching cultures of south Texas and northern Mexico have been a consuming interest of mine for three-quarters of a century. It began at Benjamin Franklin Elementary School in Wichita Falls. My family had ranching interests in north Texas and my closest companion was a spotted mare named Princess. Yet my childhood was distant and distinct from the ranching settlements along the Rio Grande, that thin life-giving space that served to unify the residents of Texas and Mexico for centuries. My encounter with that world was stimulated reading the tales and narratives of J. Frank Dobie. I first read *On the Open Range,* which he wrote for a youthful audience and which was wisely adopted by the State of Texas as a supplementary textbook, in 1933. On my own, I then read *Vaquero of the Brush Country* and *Coronado's Children* before pursuing other southwestern authors.

The stories that Dobie collected were filled with the romance that accompanies the delights and challenges of fieldwork, a romance that cannot be found in an Internet search. I would wait three decades before having an experience as memorable as those shared by Mr. Dobie. In the summer of 1961, as I sought to unlock the secrets of the historic Spanish settlements that had been inundated beneath the waters of the Falcón Reservoir in 1953, I had an unforgettable encounter with Gifredo Muñoz. To give life to these structures, it was necessary to gain insights about the families who had dwelt in these challenging environs, some of whom could trace their holdings back two hundred years to Spanish land grants. As in many traditional societies in which newcomers are viewed with caution, the intercession of a well-regarded person is mandatory in gaining the cooperation of informants. Because of my curiosity about a place known as Cuevitas and the cultural makeup of its entire region, a friend advised: "Go to a place called Randado. The dogs are friendly. Knock on the door. A man named de la Garza will open the door. He will tell you how to look for these things." It was after dark when I reached Randado but I found the man and did as he advised. "Drive south until you see a little pile of rocks on the right side of the road. Stop there and call out the name Muñoz." As an afterthought, he asked, "Do you speak Spanish?" "Más o menos," I replied. Also he advised "never make notes or use a tape recorder." During the drive down this seldom-traveled road, I was fascinated by the wildlife along the right-of-way—foraging coyotes, a great owl that almost hit my windshield, and small creatures either hunting or being hunted.

The night was pitch black due to a dense, low cloud cover, but my headlights picked out the rock pile. Behind the clouds was a full moon that penetrated at several points in the landscape like a reversed aerial spotlight. However, without the moonlight, I could not see my hand before my face. There was nothing by the rock pile, so I shouted "Muñoz," and again "Muñoz." A little dog came out, sniffed my pants leg, then disappeared back into the brushy darkness. Shortly I could see the glow of what appeared to be a kerosene lantern faintly illuminating a window half-hidden in the brush. Then Muñoz and two joyously barking dogs were revealed by the headlights. I stated the reason for my visit. The dogs were restless. "We need to go where we can sit," he said. So I followed the sound of his voice blindly, knowing by the smells that I was in a corral. When I was instructed to sit, my hands found a large mesquite log. There was a small commotion at my feet—glistening eyes. Snakes? At that point, the moon spotlighted the scene. At my feet were the two dogs on their sides, legs outstretched encircling a pool of sand. On the sand, with glistening eyes, sat a group of Pekin ducklings. "The coyotes will get them if the dogs are not here," he remarked. We all listened attentively, the dogs, the ducklings, and I as Gifredo Muñoz described the ranches, settlements, problems with the Indians, and how people built things that helped them cope with their dilemmas—how they survived at all. He described Cuevitas, that is "little caves," and how the caves were used as dwellings during the early years of the settlements. As he suggested, I returned during daylight hours to see the buildings, the corrals, and the cemetery that he had described. On one ruined structure, I found the name "Muñoz" carved on the *viga major*, the main roof beam.

Knowledge of historic Spanish settlements located in Starr and Zapata counties on the Texas side of the Rio Grande, sites that were inundated beneath the waters of the Falcón Reservoir in 1953, came to me in a circuitous way. The survey work, begun in 1948 and concluded in January 1953, that yielded this information had been undertaken by agencies concerned with the destruction of cultural artifacts within the reservoir area caused by the impounding of water as well as the displacement of the population. These agencies included the Smithsonian Institution through its River Basin Surveys, the Santa Fe office of the National Park Service, as well as interdisciplinary entities of the University of Texas at Austin. The salvage field studies and the participants involved are summarized in the appendix.

My involvement began in the summer of 1961 when I entered into a contract with the National Park Service through their western office in San Francisco. My charge was to measure and document Mission San Antonio de Valero, the Alamo, in San Antonio, Texas, first begun in 1744, for the Historic American Buildings Survey (HABS). The other four Spanish colonial missions spaced at intervals along the San Antonio River had been documented by HABS in 1934–36 as part of a Depression-era relief program for architects. Architect Marvin Eickenroht was district officer for the program in Texas from 1933 until his death in 1969, although between World War II and into the mid-1950s no HABS recording projects were undertaken. When the program was belatedly reinstituted in Texas, the Alamo was Eickenroht's top priority. The disproportionate allocation of funds to projects on the East and West Coasts caused the delay.

In the postwar period, HABS recording projects largely relied on summer field teams of architecture students under the direct supervision of university professors of architecture. At the time, I was an associate professor in the School of Architecture at the University of Texas at Austin. For my field team, I enlisted the services of two talented and well-motivated students, José G. Jiménez and James Emmrich. The Daughters of the Republic of Texas (DRT), who had been custodians of the Alamo since 1905, had earlier denied HABS permission to measure and document this major landmark. They now acquiesced. In addition, they approved our request to conduct an archaeological investigation of the foundations in order to diagnose cracks and deterioration of the walls of the building. A trove of eighteenth-century artifacts had also recently been revealed when groundskeepers installed a sprinkler system. Although I had taken introductory courses in anthropology with the idea of getting a doctorate in archaeology, I had not attained the competence to undertake such an important dig.

Edward B. Jelks, then executive director of the Texas Archaeological Salvage Project based at the Balcones Research Center at UT-Austin, now called the J. J. Pickle Research Campus, was selected to conduct the archaeological research and was keen to get started. He was on the road to San Antonio to begin work when the DRT withdrew the necessary authorization for his work. (Since 1966, archaeological investigations at the Alamo have been permitted, yielding invaluable information.) As an alternative we studied the foundation problems of nearby buildings, such as the Crockett Hotel and the U.S. post office. The two students and I completed seventeen sheets of drawings including site plans, building plans, elevations, sections, and details as well as photographic documentation—designated by HABS as TEX 318.

During my initial encounter with Dr. Jelks, however, he extended a challenge that would redirect the course of my life's work in a productive and exciting way. The archaeological field studies of historic sites soon to be flooded by the Falcón Reservoir had never been evaluated and published. As was then the norm, the primary interest of the investigators was in prehistoric Native Americans who occupied the area prior to the arrival of Spanish colonists. These data had lain in the files at the Balcones Research Center for nine years. I accepted the challenge to complete the unfinished architectural studies utilizing this material. Were it not for photographs made in the course of salvage surveys as well as the notebooks compiled by Joe F. Cason, which included field sketches, measurements, architectural clues, and genealogical records, this information would have been forever lost. Copies of all documents as well as photographs were made available to me by Jelks and Dee Ann Suhm Story, with the further assistance of Terissa Lazicki. Dr. Story was executive director of the Texas Archaeological Research Laboratory (TARL) from its formation in 1963 until 1987, when she was succeeded by Professor Thomas Hester. TARL continues to be a valuable resource.

Having completed our work at the Alamo, we were given permission by the National Park Service to use unexpended grant money for HABS documentation on buildings of our own choosing. Our team of three spent the remaining weeks of the summer in the borderlands along the Rio Grande. For me, this was a return trip. Some months earlier, I had journeyed from Austin to Roma in Starr County in order to evaluate a student research paper. Evan Hintner, a native of the Rio Grande Valley, had written about the Nestor Saénz store (1884) on Hidalgo Street and Juarez Alley in Roma, a once flourishing trade center that was head of navigation on the Rio Grande until 1907. This was my first encounter with the work of Heinrich Portscheller, the German-born architect, builder, and brickmaker who was responsible for this and other landmarks in Roma, Rio Grande City, and Laredo.

Almost a quarter century earlier, in my fifteenth summer, I had traveled with an older friend from Wichita Falls to Laredo thence along the Rio Grande to Port Isabel, trailing a seventeen-foot sailboat. When we made a fueling stop at San Ygnacio, the townspeople gathered to learn of our planned sailing adventure as well as to examine the boat. I inquired whether I might cash a twenty dollar traveler's check in order to pay my share of our expenses. Of course. A young boy dashed off and soon returned with the sum in small change. My high school Spanish would serve us well. And when we reached the coast, the Hispanic fishermen we met were as interested in our modern boat as we were by their traditional scow sloops. So we sailed one of their boats and they sailed ours—my first borderlands sailing experience. (A shoal-draft, sail-powered wooden vessel, the scow evolved to meet the unique conditions of the Texas coast. With a sloop-rigged single mast and a centerboard, it was maneuverable in the variable winds of the coastal lagoons. Like borderlands buildings, these vessels were easy to build and, because they were well-adapted to the challenging environment, their design remained consistent from 1850 until 1952, according to Reed Lewis, research volunteer with the Texas Maritime Museum in Rockport, where a replica of the scow sloop is now on display.)

Before our homeward journey, I voiced regret that we had not enjoyed the shrimp for which the Gulf Coast is famous. A fisherman overheard my comment and spent most of the night fulfilling my wish. A supply of fresh shrimp that had been boiled in sea water was his parting gift.

In Roma, when our team undertook the measured drawings and documentation of the Nestor Saénz store (1884/TEX 3129, also spelled Saéns), Evan Hintner joined his classmates, Jiménez and Emmrich. In Roma, we also produced photo-data books for the Leocadio Leandro Garcia house (ca. 1850/TEX 3131) and two other Portscheller buildings, the Manuel Guerra residence and store (1884/TEX 3146) and the residence of Rafael Garcia Ramírez (ca. 1880/TEX 3134). In our investigation of the Church of

Our Lady of Refuge of Sinners there (1854/TEX 3135), I first learned about the designer Father Pierre Keralum. A native of Brittany, Keralum studied architecture in Paris before becoming a missionary of the Oblates of Mary Immaculate assigned to the mission at Roma. In Brownsville, research indicated that the Church of the Immaculate Conception (1859/TEX 3139) was also designed by Keralum. A photo-data book was assembled for a fourth Portscheller building, the Silverio de la Peña drugstore and post office in Rio Grande City (1886/TEX 3136). In Cuevitas in Jim Hogg County, yet another photo-data book was prepared for the Eugenio Rodriquez house and post office (ca. 1850+/TEX3138). Using information in Joe Cason's notebooks, I also documented the José Ramírez house at Ramireño (ca.1781/TEX 3130), which had been inundated by the Falcón Reservoir. When our summer's work was finalized during the fall semester back at the university and submitted to HABS, St. George Pope, the director, was favorably impressed by our contractual work on the Alamo and the additional work that was accomplished as *pilón*.

In terms of research opportunities, the borderlands are rich in architectural treasures waiting to be discovered. However, we were not the first. In the mid 1930s, HABS teams under the direction of Marvin Eickenroht preceded us and produced measured drawings and documentation of buildings in San Ignacio, Rio Grande City, the Brownsville vicinity, and ranch buildings later flooded by the Falcón Reservoir.

Recording the built environment for the Historic American Buildings Survey was just a beginning. I now had enough compelling interests to fill several lifetimes: Heinrich Portscheller and Father Pierre Keralum, both European-born and -trained, and the builders of vernacular buildings in the borderlands whose names we have yet to learn.

A good start was made on my borderlands research that summer of 1961 and through the next academic year. Notable historians continued to mentor me in the ways of the region, directing me to those with knowledge of all that had gone before—like Gifredo Muñoz. Florence Johnson Scott was just such a person; she would be a most enthusiastic and knowledgeable sponsor and friend. Educator, historian, and civic leader, Mrs. Scott devoted her energies to raising the educational standards of Starr County for more than three decades. *The Historical Heritage of the Rio Grande Valley* was the first of her several published works concerning the borderlands. Another resource was Mercurio Martinez, the tax assessor of Starr County, who coauthored *The Kingdom of Zapata* with Virgil Lott. For many years, Lott was a member of the U.S. Customs Border Patrol, the service usually known as the "river riders."

Rafaela Barrera, the high school history teacher in Roma, invited me to tell her students of my interest in and admiration for the special places in which they lived—which they took for granted. This enhanced my credibility as did a similar presentation before a community group in Rio Grande City. Then professional opportunities too challenging to shirk came my way. For more than a decade, from the fall of 1962 until 1973, I endeavored, with varying degrees of success, to make contributions in the areas of architectural education and historic preservation. But the idea of completing a report on the significant buildings that were inundated by the Falcón Reservoir was never far from my thoughts. Using documentation recorded in the course of archaeological field studies from 1949 to 1952, I continued to make analytical drawings and gather historical information. The work was self-assigned and unfunded.

In 1973 I returned to Austin and reestablished my architectural practice. Most recently, I had been resident architect at Colonial Williamsburg and had a working relationship with the archaeological community there. As fate would have it, the first big job upon my return to Texas was back in Virginia. I was selected by the National Park Service for a bicentennial project in Yorktown, site of the climactic battle of the American Revolution. The work, which was coordinated with archaeologists at the College of William and Mary, involved the restoration and redevelopment of the grounds, outbuildings, and landscape features of the Nelson block to their eighteenth-century condition. The Georgian-style brick mansion, built in 1729 for the Nelson family, and the surrounding grounds, which occupied a full block, had been acquired by the National Park Service in 1968. Lord Cornwallis, the British general who surrendered to Washington at the Battle of Yorktown, had used the house as his headquarters. In acknowledgment of the role the French played in the American victory, our assignment included the reconstruction of the French redoubt and artillery at the second siege line. Richard Ryan, the first person I hired for the new office, was involved with the work in Yorktown. Richard, who had graduated at the top of his class in architecture from the University of Texas at Austin, was soon joined by Katherine Livingston, a recent graduate of the same program.

With the work in Virginia completed, the office was soon engaged in an enterprise of which I had long dreamed: the publication of *Historic Architecture of Texas: The Falcón Reservoir*. The Texas Historical Commission needed a bicentennial project and this was an expeditious choice. Truett Latimer, executive director of the commission (1965–81), and Joe Williams, director of the National Register of Historic Places for Texas (1974–79), were aware that the manuscript and illustrative material for what came to be known as the Falcón report needed only to be put in final form. Seizing the opportunity, they arranged for a modest grant in October 1975. The material was to be ready for publication by mid-December.

With a lead time of just two months, the talented and enthusiastic project staff worked long hours to complete the assignment. In addition to the drawings I had already completed, Richard Ryan prepared elevations and an analytical perspective for the house at Clareño. He also worked many nights in a rented darkroom, making prints from negatives of the Falcón material. As these were in a deteriorated condition after a quarter century, Christopher Williams, a freelance technician, restored and enhanced prints for the publication. The drawing of the Shrine at the Well at El Tigre was executed by Katherine Livingston. We also benefited from the expertise of consultant and staff participant Marsha Jackson, a historian whose area of interest is the cultural heritage of the borderlands. During her formative years growing up in Laredo, her father, James F. Jackson, was an attorney for the International Boundary and Water Commission and handled condemnation proceedings related to the building of the Falcón Reservoir.

The tight deadline set by the state printing office was met. Then a job with higher priority sidetracked the historical commission's bicentennial project. Finally, a limited edition of five hundred books was released and distributed free of charge. I hand-delivered copies throughout the focus region to recipients who were grateful to have tangible evidence of their lost world. Of course, the work was not finished, indeed, never will be. One mission of my architectural practice is the documentation of cultural assets that are fading, even vanishing, and every opportunity is seized, including enlisting students of architecture in this quest. I had returned to the UT School of Architecture as an adjunct professor in the historic preservation program from 1976 to 1985.

Around 1980 my office received two commissions for projects upstream on the Rio Grande. For the Texas Historical Commission, the first was a restoration plan for Mission Socorro (1840s) in the El Paso area—a plan that was derailed by local politicos who sanctioned a tragic intervention. The exterior of the adobe church was cement plastered, which trapped moisture and led to structural deterioration. In 1999 Cornerstones Community Partnerships of Santa Fe, New Mexico, began the lengthy restoration process. The measured drawings of Socorro that I made with Jorge Pardo and Logan Wagner have, at long last, been put to use. For Texas Parks and Wildlife, the second commission—the restoration of the Magoffin house built in 1875 in El Paso—was a more productive experience. Katherine Livingston also made a series of drawings inspired by the Hispanic antique furniture in an area dealer's collection.

As is desirable, those who came into the office as intern architects moved forward professionally and were replaced by others. When work was slow, skill-enhancing exercises often involved borderlands material. Jorge Pardo produced a series of drawings of architectural details based on photographs made before the completion of the Falcón Reservoir as well as those I made in the course of my ongoing investigations. (A selection of these are reproduced in the introduction.) Laurie Limbacher, a graduate of Texas A&M University, made an analytical perspective drawing of the Treviño fortified house in San Ignacio, using information gathered by the 1936 Historic American Buildings Survey. Zeb Rike, an architect from McAllen, Texas, who had been involved with the HABS programs in South Texas in the 1930s under Marvin Eickenroht, was a source of information and insights.

Then in 1983, Anselmo Treviño, principal of the A. L. Benavides Elementary School in San Ignacio, called with the news that the town of Guerrero Viejo in the state of Tamaulipas on the Mexican side of the reservoir had been partially exposed.

The lake level, already low because of decreased precipitation, had temporarily been lowered even further to permit a highway construction project. My wife and I were en route the next day and made our first visit to Guerrero Viejo with Mary Simpson of Zapata, a knowledgeable hunters' guide and businesswoman. Extensive large format photographs were made of the architecture and its sculptural ornament then and on subsequent visits soon thereafter. It was at this time that we met Jean Fish and her husband, Colonel Robert Fish, who were making significant contributions to historical research in the region. The town remained above the waterline for three years until the heavy rains of 1986 when it was again partially buried under the waters of the lake—one might say "safely buried."

When Guerrero Viejo was once more revealed during the great drought of 1996–98, the splendid Corinthian capital, still bearing its polychrome paint, and other artifacts I had earlier photographed were nowhere to be seen. Now the reservoir shrank to one-twelfth of its capacity revealing many sites including cemeteries, the remains of ranching settlements, and prehistoric sites that had been submerged for more than forty years.

At the time the river was closed at the Falcón Dam in late 1952, the projected time for the reservoir to fill had been three years, however heavy rains in the watershed forced evacuation of the area in just nine months. Precious possessions were abandoned forever. Tragically there was not even time to relocate many burials.

In 1996, under the direction of Dr. Thomas Hester, executive director of the Texas Archaeological Research Laboratory, a survey effort was mounted to assess the damage and determine how to stop the looters and commercial artifact collectors who were pillaging sites on the parched floor of the reservoir. Dr. Hester's team included personnel from the National Park Service, the Texas Historical Commission, several state archaeological groups, and myself.

Accounts published by newspapers near and far told the tragic story: the looters proved to be more adept than the preservationists. Only with the break in the drought in the first years of the new century, with flooding in Mexico and heavy rains up and down the Rio Grande Valley, which replenished the reservoir, would the desecration cease. Again, "safely buried," but for how long?

For updated information, visit www.texasbeyondhistory.net/falcon. Texas beyond History: Falcon Reservoir is a Web site maintained by the Texas Archaeological Research Laboratory.

Worthy of mention are the subsequent accomplishments of the men and women who passed through my office and were involved with the borderlands material. A few high points will suffice. Richard Ryan was an architect with the Main Street program of the Texas Historical Commission from 1982 to 2000. Based in Fort Worth, Katherine Livingston practiced architecture, then earned an MBA degree. She is now a liaison between school districts and is involved in their building campaigns. Marsha Jackson was registrar of archaeological sites for the state of New Mexico from 1977 to 1987, followed by thirteen years as deputy director of the Museum of New Mexico in Santa Fe. Laurie Limbacher was director of design and project architect with the State Preservation Board for the Texas Capitol Preservation and Expansion Project. Jorge Pardo has been art and design manager for the Metropolitan Transportation Authority for the city of Los Angeles since 1990. E. Logan Wagner, Ph.D., draws upon his knowledge of both traditional and contemporary Mexican architecture as architect, builder, and author.

# Lost Architecture of the Rio Grande Borderlands

Rivers cradle civilizations. Rivers nourish life, providing moisture and fresh soil in the rhythmic pulses of time. The Rio Grande, whose headwaters rise in southwestern Colorado, flows southward through New Mexico and forms the boundary between Texas and Mexico—extending from El Paso to the Gulf of Mexico. Like the Nile, the Rio Grande must be viewed as a central, dominant, life-enhancing region, varying in width, and curving through an otherwise severe landscape. While the river may be understood on the maps and at the border checkpoints as the firm boundary between the United States and Mexico, this thin, life-giving resource has served to unify its residents as one culture. The river exists as one clearly defined geographic entity, unifying rather than dividing, a common central stream toward which life has focused for millennia.[1]

In an attempt to stabilize the Texas-Mexican Rio Grande borderlands, José de Escandón initiated a colonization scheme during the middle of the eighteenth century. The central body of this book—a revised version of *Historic Architecture of Texas: The Falcón Reservoir*—documents that epic achievement and the tragic aftermath. Many of the sites from the Escandón effort now rest beneath the waters of the Falcón reservoir. The parameters of this study are those towns and settlements. In addition, a photographic essay of Guerrero Viejo (Revilla) in the state of Tamaulipas on the Mexican side, which shared their fate, is included in the epilogue. That the earliest settlers survived at all bears witness to the resilience of the human spirit. Intense heat and interminable droughts, virulent diseases and merciless attacks by predatory men, even starvation, were facts of existence as were floods without warning and the more predictable rush of high water each spring caused by the snowmelt in the mountains of Colorado. The Rio Grande has been known by many names over time and in different parts of its course. By 1598 the Spaniards were calling the stretch of our concern—the lower course—the Rio Bravo and in Mexico today it is called the Rio Bravo del Norte. Translations of the term, "bravo" include wild, ferocious, harsh, and ill-tempered. The river was also called the Rio Caudaloso, that is, carrying much water.[2]

Drought, flood, and disease were among the accepted hazards of everyday life. The unchanging visual environment provided stability for those who coexisted with its hazards. Long association with the landscape—buildings, pastures, terraces of corn above the river—maintained continuity through the generations and was inte-

gral to the character of the culture. The structures that defined the people's lives and helped them cope with their environment is the focus of this book.

Agriculture supported by irrigation, Escandón's original vision for the region, was not feasible due to the aridity of the land and the quality of the soil.[3] Water was so rapidly absorbed that it could not be carried any great distance. Instead, a frontier ranching province evolved that brought great wealth to a fortunate few. All *porciones* (assigned lands) required a watering place for cattle. The individual land measurement decided on as the most practical for the jurisdictions assumed the shape of a prolonged quadrangle with the width approximately nine-thirteenths of a mile of river front, the length extending back from a certain point on the Rio Grande from eleven to sixteen miles. As a testament to the preciousness of the river, the *porciones* were often given religious names, which became the names of the ranches.

In addition to sustaining the livestock, the riparian environment provided material for building settlements and ranch sites. As Joe Cason recorded in his notebooks in about 1950, river sandstone was easily quarried along the banks of that stretch of the river—exposed in the so-called sixty-foot terrace, the first terrace above the one immediately contiguous to the river. As a construction unit, the sandstone was employed in a variety of shapes and sizes, which suggests that the stones were used without alteration, just as they were broken out of the bed rocks at the quarry, that is rubble, or *mampostería*. At the corners of buildings and at openings, a dense hard limestone characterized by well-defined horizontal cleavage was sometimes employed in buildings constructed of rubble. This technique is termed *sillar de esquina. Sillar* refers simply to a square or rectangular dressed stone, that is, ashlar.; *esquina* means "corner."[4]

The abundance of sandstone was fortuitous. Comanche and Lipan Apache bands raided the area regularly. Such raiding was reported by the first colonists and, according to local tradition, continued until the 1870s. Stone construction is not only impervious to fire but also seems to have retarded other siege mechanisms the Indian bands possessed. The defensive properties of sandstone must have served as a powerful incentive for the backbreaking labor necessary to erect the stone buildings in the early colonial period.

With the quarries above the river providing an abundant supply of sandstone, there was no need to use caliche block as at Randado or fired brick as was expedient elsewhere.[5] Certainly, brickmaking in Rio Grande City and nearby Roma was extensive after the mid-nineteenth century. (Buildings in these towns, especially those constructed by Heinrich Portscheller, master brickmaker and builder, have been a parallel subject of my research since 1961.)

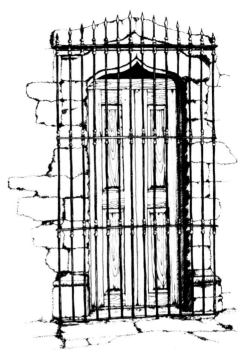

The structures that survived to the mid-twentieth century represented the final phase of a typical pioneering sequence. The transition may well have begun in a cave, as at Cuevitas, then on to a wattle-and-daub or pallisado jacal or hut (more fully described in chapter 3) and finally a permanent stone structure. Like the scow sloops built by the Hispanic fishermen on the Gulf Coast, these structures evolved to meet extreme climatic conditions. They were relatively easy to build and well-adapted to the challenging environment.

Vernacular architecture is based on common sense.[6] Who were these borderland builders who endured to provide the essentials of living? What were the skills the mason, the carpenter, and the blacksmith learned as part of their craft? Secrets of the builder's trade have traditionally been passed from father to son down through the generations, within the guild system, or by serving an apprenticeship under a master craftsman. Received wisdom is also applicable to the construction and orientation of thermally efficient buildings, knowledge known since antiquity in similar climates but often ignored today, for example, sensitivity to solar orientation—the commonsense practice of designing with nature. A typical structure in an Escandón settlement, even one of modest size, had walls thirty inches thick and eleven feet tall, thus ensuring that radiant heat from the roof would not penetrate the interior space. Tall air space also facilitated ventilation, as did the updraft through the roof scuttle, a trap door that gave access to the roof, and the chimney hood when not used for heating. Concern for air circulation was critical, early on, because there were no windows. Even had glass been available, security would have dictated the absence of windows. This would change in the mid-nineteenth century, a more peaceful time. Glass and manufactured window frames arrived with the advent of Mississippi trading practices extended by steamboats hauling goods as far up the Rio Grande as Roma.

The wall height was also designed for defense. Marauders on horseback could not jump on the roof and gain entry through the roof scuttle. And the parapeted roof of-

fered protection from attack. Finally, there was a formidable doorway. Usually screened by just a curtain, it had a heavy wooden door that could be closed if necessary. A rider in a bent position could ride a horse through such a doorway, and in times of siege, the livestock was brought into the house.

In attempting to identify the contributions of these historic people—a unique type of cultural spirit—one notes characteristics such as fortitude, character, courage, stability, and reverence are evident. Buildings and tombstones that survived for two centuries were then sacrificed in the name of progress. Mexico and the United States agreed by the document known as the U.S.-Mexico Water Treaty of 1944 to build a series of international dams across the Rio Grande for the purposes of flood control, crop irrigation, recreation, and the generation of hydroelectric power.[7] The treaty also established the International Boundary and Water Commission to own and operate these projects. Earlier failed attempts to deal with boundary and water issues along the Rio Grande dated back to 1882.

Planned to harness the waters of the Rio Grande below Laredo, the dam that would contain the International Falcón Reservoir was completed in April 1954, with deliberate empoundment begun on August 25, 1953. When at maximum elevation, the reservoir is bounded by Starr and Zapata counties in Texas and the city of Nuevo Ciudad Guerrero in Tamaulipas in Mexico. While the subsurface bearing capacity of the site ultimately selected near historic Rancho Falcón was superior to many others, the deciding factor for the location of the dam was the advantageous haul distance, that is the proximity of sufficient soil to fill the five-mile-long earthen and concrete embankment. Originally called the "lowermost dam," the official name, Falcón Reservoir, was taken from Rancho Falcón, the ranch nearest the dam.

The place, first known as El Ramireño de Abajo, was founded by José Clemente Ramírez who, in 1790, married María Rita de la Garza Falcón, thereby uniting two of the area's most distinguished families. In 1915, the name of the ranching settlement was changed to Falcón in honor of the wife of the founder. And quite appropriately. According to legend, the beautiful Rita de la Garza Falcón, widowed early, saved the ranch and the family fortunes by manufacturing soap that she sold in the markets of northern Mexico.

Because of a prolonged drought, officials thought it would take several years for the reservoir to fill. So the dam was closed before the government paid those who had been dispossessed of their land. But in August 1953, the rains came and the five-hundred-year floodplain was quickly reached. In the pouring rain, the waters swallowed up the old settlements of Zapata, Lopeño, Ramireño, Uribeño, Tepezán, Clareño and others. (See Fig. 12 for settlements within the reservoir boundaries.) And the families who had lived in these places down through the generations were driven from their ancestral homes, often forced to abandon their life's possessions. More than half the population of Zapata County was displaced; 115,000 acres of ranchland was flooded. After condemning these historic settlements, the government refused to pay full price for homes and belongings because they were "no longer usable." A tent city that would be home for eighteen months to thousands of refugees was the only option they were offered. In contrast, Nuevo Ciudad Guerrero, built by the Mexican government, was ready for the displaced citizens of Guerrero Viejo; uninspiring at best but with modern conveniences.

Amid the desolation, one decision would forevermore stand as a reminder of all that was lost. San Ygnacio, also spelled Ignacio, had been scheduled for demolition along with the Escandón settlements. In April 1951, however, several hundred residents petitioned to have their lands excluded from condemnation proceedings on the grounds that their town site was sufficiently high above the maximum reservoir surface line. Recorded previous floods dating back to 1865 had never reached any part of their community. The request was granted. Then capricious Mother Nature sent the great flood of 1953, causing widespread damage.[8]

San Ygnacio, the oldest surviving town in Zapata County, is sited on a bluff overlooking the Rio Grande, thirty miles south of Laredo. It was settled in 1830 by former residents of Revilla/Guerrero Viejo in Tamaulipas under the leadership of Jesús Treviño who had ranching interests on both sides of the river. It was named for Saint Ignatius Loyola. Blas María Uribe, who married Treviño's daughter Juliana Treviño de Uribe also moved his family from Revilla to the Treviño outpost at Rancho San Ygnacio. The original town plat was laid out in a grid that followed the cardinal directions and was organized around a central plaza as at Revilla. The scale, building style, and construction techniques also followed the same traditions but with less ornamentation.

As described by I. T. Frary in his article "Picturesque Towns of the Border Land," in the *Architectural Record* of April 1919, "the houses [of San Ygnacio] are built mostly of stone, plastered over and whitewashed, and against their white walls are contrasted the painted doors and window casings, which are invariably bright blue in color . . . and are like those of Southern European villages, bare and plain, except for an occasional touch of ornament about the doors and windows, and with here and there an example whose walls are enriched with ornamental stucco." The au-

**1.** San Ignacio, Texas, "Picturesque streets." Reprinted from I. T. Frary, "Picturesque Towns of the Border Land," *Architectural Record* (April 1919), a publication of the McGraw-Hill Companies, Inc. Supplied by publisher.

thor especially admired the beautiful window grilles of wrought iron hammered out upon the anvil in the local blacksmith shop.[9] (See Figs. 1–3.)

Most of the town is now included in the San Ygnacio Historic District, listed on the National Register of Historic Places in 1973 with boundary expansion in 1997. The district comprises the earliest development at the river's edge, the blocks correlating to the original town plat. This acknowledgment is significant because it is the only South Texas community that still retains a large number of the typical sandstone structures once numerous but lost in 1953.

The premier example of traditional architecture in San Ignacio is the Jesús Treviño–Blas Uribe Rancho, a sandstone house begun about 1830 by Jesús Treviño, which was designated in 1998 by the National Park Service as a National Historic Landmark. The statement of significance is as follows:

> The Jesús Treviño-Blas Uribe Rancho is an exceptional survivor of vernacular Mexican architectural and ranching traditions on the northern, or American, side of the Rio Grande [Fig. 4]. Evolving from a simple one-room shelter, built ca.

2. San Ignacio, Texas, "A brave showing of paneling." I. T. Frary, "Picturesque Towns of the Border Land," *Architectural Record* (April 1919), a publication of the McGraw-Hill Companies, Inc. Supplied by publisher.

1830 by Jesús Treviño, who maintained his principal residence in Mexico, the complex grew in four, possibly five building campaigns, into a large ranch head-quarters forming an enclosed quadrangle. Although the last addition dates to 1871, traditional building patterns were maintained, illustrating the persistence of Hispanic culture along the borderlands long after Texas had become part of the United States. Largely in original condition, the complex vividly portrays the Mexican/Texan frontier experience.[10]

The structure has, traditionally, also been referred to as Fort Treviño—with good cause. Townspeople and those from outlying ranches gathered within its defensible wall in times of danger. *Troneras*—loopholes embracing a controlled field of fire from weapons within—are still much in evidence. In addition to marauding Indian bands that would continue to be a threat until the late 1870s, border troubles along the Rio Grande had escalated dramatically by the mid-nineteenth century.

The conflict between the United States and Mexico, known as the Mexican War (1846–48), had its roots in the U.S. annexation of Texas, countered by Mexico's

**3.** San Ignacio, Texas, "Beautiful window grilles or *rejas*." I. T. Frary, "Picturesque Towns of the Border Land," *Architectural Record* (April 1919), a publication of the McGraw-Hill Companies, Inc. Supplied by publisher.

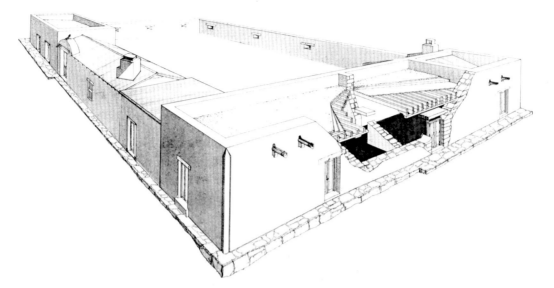

**4.** Analytical perspective drawing of the Jesús Treviño–Blas Uribe fortified house in San Ignacio, Texas, by Laurie Limbacher.

refusals to cede Texas. Under the 1848 Treaty of Guadalupe Hidalgo, lands that had been held in common for more than a century by descendants of Spanish grantees were expropriated from Texans of Mexican descent, that is, Tejanos, most of whom were familiar with neither the American judicial system nor the English language.[11] The secession of Texas during the Civil War also deeply divided Mexican Americans. And there was ongoing political upheaval and revolution in Mexico that spilled across the river. Into the void created by bitterness and instability rode the bandidos. The protection of the border area where outlawry was rampant became the top priority of the U.S. Army. With the opening of Fort Sam Houston in 1879, San Antonio was the central point from which troops could radiate along the entire Rio Grande frontier from Fort Brown at Brownsville upriver five hundred miles to the Pecos River.[12] When the bandits swept the region, pillaging and killing, they often stole fine furniture that had been imported from France through the Port of New Orleans then up the Rio Grande to Roma for delivery to borderlands households. There was a ready market south of the border—warehouses in Matamoros were filled with these treasures.[13]

Reasons for caring? "What is past is prologue." So observed William Shakespeare in *The Tempest*. Rather than mourn a lost world buried beneath the waters of the Falcón Reservoir, let us pay homage to their achievement by salvaging what is applicable to the future. Consider lessons that can be learned about energy efficiency

**5.** Leal Juarez house, view southwest; Tepezán, Zapata County, Texas. Photograph attributed to Edward B. Jelks (Fr 38, 35-mm neg), TARL catalog reference 41ZP87 (1).

and the sustainable use of building materials in extreme climates. And what of their aesthetic design qualities that were shaped by response to the environment? Working with limited resources, the vernacular is capable of great dignity—of enviable simplicity—even of elegance.

The spirit, as well as the substance, of these important elements of the built heritage of Texas has inspired architectural achievement in recent decades. To cite one example near San Antonio: a house for David Straus on a ranch about a dozen miles east of Castroville on the Medina River.[14] For a client who descends from a pioneer saddler, the architectural firm of O'Neill and Perez (until 1984), with project architect Steve Tillotson, was able to give expression to their research interests in indigenous structures. The Leal Juarez house that once stood near Tepezán, a settlement inundated by the reservoir in 1953, provided key design details for the compound (Fig. 5). This modern interpretation of historic antecedents has thick masonry walls, a steeply pitched roof with parapeted gable ends, exposed wood decking that makes up the high ceilings, and massive chimneys found attached to even the most humble borderlands structures such as the Tepezán house. Because the Straus-Medina Hereford Ranch is blessed with an artesian well, the design concept centers on water that is channeled into an acequia and irrigates both gardens and orchard before forming a small waterfall and flowing into the Medina River.

**6.** Built on the edge of the Medina River, this house on the Straus-Medina Hereford Ranch near Castroville, Texas, was inspired by regional precedents. Project architect Stephen Tillotson—with the firm of O'Neill and Perez—found design inspiration in the Leal Juarez house near Tepezán, which included thick walls, parapeted gables, and strong geometric chimneys. The dwelling seems to come out of the earth. Photograph by the author, 1986.

**7.** A modern version of the traditional summer kitchen and patio; the chimney serves as a large barbeque grill. Photograph by the author, 1986.

**8.** The basic concept of the David Straus ranch house centers on water.
A check dam downstream forms a small lake that becomes part of the view
from the living room. Photograph by the author, 1986.

Responding to the geometric shapes of the Leal Juarez house, Tillotson developed a plan for the main house where three long rectangular units join to center on the dining room. The dining and living room areas open onto a loggia where sitting out-of-doors in a shaded area enjoying the view as the shadows change is a delight.

There is in this house a quality that architectural critics have described as a "sense of fitness." This is partly attributable to the background sound of running water or because its solid, well-proportioned walls give a sense of security. But chiefly it comes from the fact that the house grew quite consciously out of a historical context, and that it partakes of the spiritual qualities of its site. It is this kind of "fitness" that grows with age, as house and site give and take from one another over the years, until it is impossible to imagine that they ever had separate lives.

The Rio Grande flows through a region that was known during the Spanish colonial period as Nuevo Santander. Following the initial Spanish exploration of the New World in the sixteenth century, this vast area remained unsettled and virtually unexplored for two and a half centuries. However, after the first quarter of the eighteenth century, the viceregal government in Mexico began procedures to stabilize the territory. Four concerns stimulated colonization. First, Spanish authorities were shocked by knowledge that the French had attempted settlement on Garcitas Creek, which flows into Matagorda Bay, a major bay on the Texas coast protected by the Matagorda Peninsula from the tides and storms of the Gulf of Mexico. News of this encroachment was like a fire bell in the night.[1] Though the French settlement under La Salle was unsuccessful, to Spanish minds, the attempted occupation was an invasion of their territory. During the same period, the British had occupied the Bahamas and Jamaica. Spanish settlements in the province of Nuevo Santander would provide resistance against continued expansion by foreign entities.

Second, the Spaniards had interests in eastern Texas that were threatened by French activity in Louisiana. To protect these interests as well as to maintain lines of communication between regions remote to Mexico City, it was considered desirable to establish a linkage between proposed colonies in unsettled regions.[2] A Rio Grande settlement would be a crucial part of this effort.

Third, the aboriginal occupants of the Rio Grande, which were becoming increasingly hostile, posed a particularly severe threat. Spanish chronicles from as early as 1573 display intimate knowledge of the indigenous peoples of northern Tamaulipas and southern Texas.[3]

Fourth, mineral wealth was ever a motivation for the Spaniards. Rumors of precious ore in the Tamaulipas Mountains provided another incentive for colonization. A more tangible wealth existed in the form of salt. The Rio Salado, which joins the Rio Grande near Revilla/Guerrero Viejo, had been well named. Aboriginal salt trails in northern Hidalgo County, Texas, had been identified since earliest times, and the towns in northern Mexico received salt from this area long before the Rio Grande was settled. One river crossing on the old salt trail is known to have been located at present-day Roma. Another was a sandstone reef five miles upstream from Roma known as the Paso de los Indios.[4]

A royal *cedula* issued on the tenth day of July, 1739, ordered colonization of the last part of northeastern Mexico to be conquered and effectively occupied. The task was assigned to a junta composed not only of the viceroy and members of the *auden-cia* in Mexico City but also of people informed on matters concerning colonization and the area to be settled.[5]

## JOSÉ DE ESCANDÓN

José de Escandón was commissioned on the third of September, 1746, to head the colonization attempt and, one year later, was given the rank of captain-general and governor of the new territory. As sergeant of the Querétaro militia since 1734, he had opposed indigenous war parties who were carrying their raiding forays into the streets of Spanish-Mexican villages. Escandón followed the invaders through several campaigns into the most inaccessible parts of the Sierra Gorda; he captured and punished their leaders while at the same time correcting ingrained abuses by Spanish officialdom. Through these actions, Escandón not only gained the respect of the soldiers who followed him but also gratitude and support from the pacified tribes.

The province of Nuevo Santander, founded by Escandón in 1746, was named for his native province in Spain.[6] The colony was initially called Colonia de la Costa del Seno Mexicano (Gulf Coast Colony). Included was the area between present-day Tampico on the south and the Bay of Espíritu Santo on the north—near Matagorda Bay on the Texas coast—and from the Gulf of Mexico to the mountainous boundary formed by the Sierra Madre Oriental. The Rio Grande was the river with the greatest length and the largest volume of water within the territory. It flows southeastward through the center of the region.

## THE SURVEY

A comprehensive visual survey of the entire territory was the colonizers' first task. Earlier attempts had failed to yield adequate information, sometimes because the surveyors did not survive the wilderness. Empowered by his new authority as governor of Nuevo Santander, Escandón benefited from advice of individuals who had experienced the problems encountered on the frontier. He then prepared a plan of action utilizing comprehensive information concerning native populations, rivers, mountains, and other geographic features. Data concerning a tribe of mixed breeds and Negroes dwelling near the mouth of the Rio Grande was included. How these people arrived in the area is still a matter of speculation, with wrecked slave ships a possibility. Whatever their origin, they employed spears and shields and were fearsome warriors.[7] Escandón proposed the introduction of several companies of troops, each unit responsible for accumulating information relative to their assigned portion of the hinterlands. The troops were to remain in the field for thirty days, then report simultaneously at a specified site near the mouth of the Rio Grande. According to plan, Escandón departed from Querétaro northward on the seventh of January, 1747. Other units of the expedition were ordered to depart from designated positions later in the same month and to rendezvous on the twenty-fourth of February, 1747. Though some of the units did not arrive at the appointed time and place, the difficult task was nonetheless accomplished in a short time. The comprehensive inspection of the region included parts heretofore unknown. The plan of penetration from several points on the frontier using small mobile units covering short distances proved to be excellent. Seven hundred sixty soldiers participated, without loss of life, in a survey that lasted seven weeks. A detailed report of the findings of the collaborative expedition was forwarded to the viceroy and was then integrated into plans for the distribution of settlements in the vacant landscape.

After two years of evaluation and planning, Escandón submitted his final proposal to the authorities. The settlers could now depart for the new territory. The extent of the lands proposed for inclusion is shown on a 1792 map of Sierra Gorda, including the Province of Nuevo Santander (Fig. 9). A map of Sierra Gorda redrawn from the 1792 map traces the routes followed in the survey of 1747 (Fig. 10).

### THE SETTLEMENTS

Desirable sites for fourteen settlements were designated. As civil administration was to be stressed, no presidios were proposed. The needs of colonial immigrants were one consideration in the initial site selection, but strategic domination of the Gulf Coast as well as areas occupied by the interior tribes was also a concern. The selected sites included those on the Rio Grande and two on the Nueces and San Antonio rivers. Religious concerns would be under the able care of missionaries from the College of Guadalupe de Zacatecas. The hardy, self-reliant people who were selected as colonists included Spaniards, mestizos, and mulattos.[8]

Escandón's reputation and his previous successes encouraged more volunteers than could be accommodated. A generous moving allowance of one to two hundred pesos per family as well as the promise of good land not to be taxed for ten years were surely strong additional incentives. During the provisioning phase of the operation, supplies for the colonists were accumulated at various depots. Regrettably, profiteering by officials on scarce necessities was not unknown.

On the sixteenth of November, 1748, 2,515 colonists, with 755 escorting soldiers, departed from Querétaro bound for Nuevo Santander. The spectacle of the seemingly endless columns of colonists, soldiers, wagons, stock, and pack animals was greeted with demonstrations of sympathy and enthusiasm along the way. En route, the convoy paused at a number of towns in the province of Guanajuato where additional families joined the entourage.[9]

At San Luis Potosí in early December, the moving column braved a snow storm as well as an epidemic of smallpox. On Christmas day, 1748, forty-four families were issued oxen and implements to found the small village of Santa María de Llera, the first of the new settlements in Nuevo Santander. The capital of the colony, Jiménez, approximately 125 miles south of present-day Matamoros, was founded in February 1749. The south bank of the Rio Grande was reached during the following month

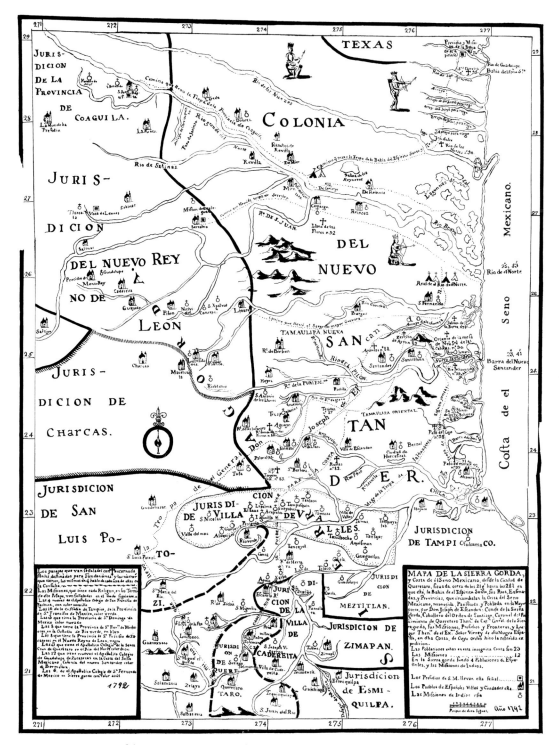

**9.** Map of the Sierra Gorda, 1792, including Nuevo Santander. Original in the Museo Nacional, Mexico.

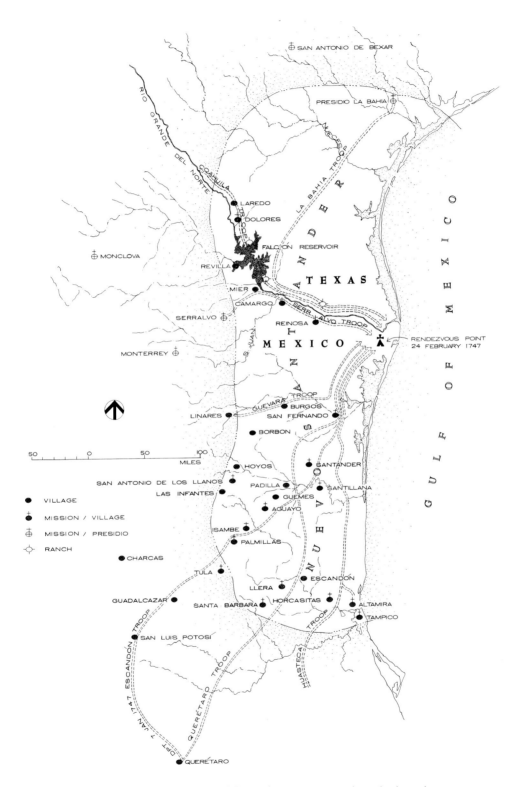

**10.** Map of Sierra Gorda showing routes followed during the 1747 survey; redrawn by the author from a 1792 map (Fig. 9).

where the *villas* (villages) of Camargo and Reinosa were established on March 5 and 14, respectively.[10]

By May 1749, Escandón was on the return route to Querétaro, but he found little time to celebrate his successful mission. His energy and aggressiveness had, in some way, offended the church hierarchy who challenged his policies. The policies survived, though months were consumed with reports to the viceroy as well as with other administrative matters. Also, because attacks on the settlements had occurred from the beginning, the civil administration was altered to include ten military squadrons for protection. Two sites, initially proposed in present-day Texas, one on the Nueces and the other on the San Antonio River, were abandoned. The Nueces settlement had, in fact, been attempted but the assigned group found the location impossible for habitation. These colonists returned southward to the Salado near the Rio Grande to await instructions that never came. When faced with the deaths of many in the party, including their captain, and with dwindling supplies, the survivors had no choice but to disperse to other areas.

Other settlements near the Rio Grande were established under different circumstances. Silver mines in northern Mexico required an extensive labor force. However, the native peoples who were forced into service were often in a state of revolt because of the severe working conditions associated with the mines. Concentrations of these often-abused laborers inspired missionaries to move northward. Their presence reduced the danger associated with those lands, making grazing of livestock possible and profitable. Prior to Escandón's entry, ranchers had moved into the area immediately south of the Rio Grande, extending their holdings out of Monterrey. There were established ranches in the area as early as 1745. Since the advantages offered by Escandón were superior to those granted by provincial administrators, these ranchers petitioned Escandón and requested permission to found permanent *villas*. Nuevo Santander would become a frontier ranching province.

One pioneer rancher, José Vasquez of Coahuila, had made grazing surveys in present-day Zapata County, Texas, and petitioned for settlement on the north bank of the Rio Grande about ten leagues northwest of Revilla. His request was granted, and Nuestra Señora de los Dolores was founded on the twenty-second of August, 1750. The site, now known as Old Dolores, or Dolores Viejo, is immediately north of present-day San Ignacio, outside the area circumscribed by the Falcón Reservoir.[11] A rancher named Vicente Guerra made a similar request. His petition permitted the ranching community of Revilla to be established on the south side of the Rio Grande near the junction of the Salado River. Revilla, now known as Guerrero Viejo, was founded on the tenth of October, 1750. The *lugar* (town) of Mier was established on the Mexican side of the river near the old salt trail crossing (Paso de Cantero). The Alamo River joins the Rio Grande near the Mier location. Natural building materials were in good supply there and the land was easily irrigated. Mier, located halfway between Camargo and Revilla, was founded on the sixth of March, 1751.

**11.** Street scene; Revilla (Guerrero Viejo), Tamaulipas, Mexico. The Hotel Flores is on the right. Photograph by Bob Humphreys, 1950 (2x2 neg), TARL catalog reference Mexico/Tamaulipas/Falcón Reservoir General (3).

Escandón was at Revilla on an inspection trip in 1754 when he received a request for the final river settlement of importance. A rancher named Tomas Sánchez petitioned to settle on the north bank of the Rio Grande near a ford known as Paso de Jacinto. Instead, Escandón encouraged Sanchez to make a second attempt to establish a *villa* on the Nueces. This attempt also met with failure and the Rio Grande was then agreed upon. Construction of new dwellings commenced at the site on the seventeenth of May, 1755. It was Escandón's desire that the place be named San Agustín de Laredo.

When Fray Vicente Santa María chronicled the accomplishments of José de Escandón, he used terms appropriate for modern chamber of commerce boosterism in describing the delights of Nuevo Santander. He wrote that the region has a "beautiful climate in a temperate zone. . . . The location and position are without doubt the most suitable for any undertaking one wishes. The appearance is beautiful and clean; its land is adapted for everything; it is near to materials for the construction of even magnificent buildings, if they should be wished; and the abundant streams of crystal, healthy water, are distributed for use . . . all of which make it, in my opinion, a place without comparison." He was forced to admit that it is "in some parts inclined to be hot." He goes on to mention that portions of the land contain "thorny and most pernicious shrubs . . . now innumerable, and they cover and render unfit for service the fields and even the highways. . . . South of the river ranches runs a valley from the eastern slopes of the sierras to the sea, a desert of more than seventy leagues . . . uninhabitable and unfitted for cultivation."[1] Descriptions unglossed by Fray Vicente's optimism are numerous. Maximilian's Austrian troops moving near Camargo in May 1866, found that "thickets of shrubs, as high as walls, lined both sides of the road, and cut off all sight of the surrounding country. . . . The road was covered inches thick with layers of dust, which, being stirred up by the hoofs of the draught-cattle, soon converted the atmosphere into visible grit. Men, horses, and vehicles lost their individuality in dress, caparison and color, and became different-sized moving heaps of the same grey indistinguishable hue."[2]

North of the Rio Grande to the Nueces River, the land is also rugged, and presented barriers for travelers. This region was assigned during the 1747 survey to the presidio of Bahía. Because of hardships encountered in the wilderness between the two rivers, Joaquin de Orobio y Basterra arrived too late for the rendezvous with Escandón. Of the hardships experienced in 1848 when going through the region to join his unit with Gen. Zachary Taylor, Lt. Richard D. Cochrane wrote to his wife: "We are at this time entering a desert, sand two inches deep and mixed with salt, water nearly so salty as not to be fit to drink. Those two days of marching were horrible. When we arrived at our camp, you could not recognize anyone, Our faces were perfectly black with dust and salt in the dust made our eyes so painful that it was with difficulty we could open our lids to see."[3] The strip of land between the Rio Grande and the Nueces was, in time, labeled the *brasada*, a dry area hot as a bed of coals containing thorny, impenetrable growth. This is beyond doubt the region where, according to legend, a famous U.S. general said that if offered a choice between living in either hell or Texas, he would prefer to live in hell and "rent out Texas."

The nature of the landscape immediately adjacent to the Rio Grande was described by another traveler who rambled both banks of the river in the summer of 1851. The French oblate missionary Emmanuel Henri Dieudonné Domenech

[walked] along a narrow pathway winding through a thick woodland. Again we crossed the Rio Grande, here both wide and deep, for it is, after receiving several tributaries—the Rio de San Juan, the Rio Álamo, and the Salado—further enlarged by the Rio Sabinos, which comes down from the Sierra Madre. . . . Now my route was a winding road between the Rio Grande and a chain of hills that issue from the Sierra Verde and other ramifications of the Rocky Mountains. At this latitude, the plains of Western Texas disappear; the country is diversified, yet its general aspect is melancholy. The mesquite tree, the acacia, the wild strawberry, the carob, and a countless family of the cactus, are the only ornaments of these arid stony hills. Sometimes your way lies on a whitish rock, which so reflects the sun's rays as almost to scorch the eyes. Should a plant succeed in working its way through some sheltered fissure more fertile than the surrounding desert, it soon expires under the devouring heat. As a compensation, however, should you meet with a ravine or stream, or more moist soil, you find the vegetation incomparably rich and fruitful. In some of these ravines I found the gigantic *polipodiums, aspleniums,* and other species of fern, which the prolonged droughts render very rare in Texas. A death-like silence prevails in this desert; even the voice of a bird, or the roar of an animal hardly ever relieves the profound silence.[4]

### SELECTION OF BUILDING SITES

Good terrace soil, abundant firewood, shade trees, and available water were considerations in the selection of building sites for individual ranches, as revealed by archaeology. Flint chips and shards of Native American pottery are often intermingled with Spanish *majolica*. This indicates that colonial sites were previously used by native inhabitants who were skilled in the selection of beneficial environments.

Lewis Mumford, whose writings on environmental planning fill volumes, reminds us that "except in the abstractions of drawings or photography, no building exists in a void."[5] Careful site planning, therefore, with studied consideration toward the physical relationship of buildings to the site and to each other is of major importance. In the examples that follow, discrimination may have been used in the selection of the sites as a whole, but the building placement on the outlying ranches was often random and haphazard—with little concern for sun and breeze orientation.

Tienda de Cuervo, in a 1757 inspection report describing the original site of Revilla, mentioned that "instead of being arranged around the customary plaza [the houses were] scattered over broad areas, typical of communities devoted to ranching."[6] Such haphazard site arrangement was inconsistent with the orderly practices generally employed by Spanish colonizers. Because of the serious planning mistakes in the Antilles, the king gave specific instructions to one Pedrarias Dávila as early as 1513: "The places chosen for settlement . . . if inland to be on a river if possible . . . good water and air, close to arable land . . . and from the beginning it should be according to definite arrangement; for the matter of setting up the *solares* [town lots] will determine the pattern of the town, both in the position of the plaza and the church. . . . If not started with form, they will never attain it."[7] Not only did Revilla lack a central plaza during its earliest period, but Mier also had a disorderly arrangement, with thirty-nine families dwelling in stone or mud *jacales* scattered over a large area, as was typical of a large ranching community. On the other hand, Camargo, the largest and most prosperous *villa* in the entire colony in 1757, consisted of houses arranged in orderly fashion around a central plaza.[8]

Neither the river towns founded so enthusiastically by Escandón nor the earliest outlying ranches rested firmly on their new foundations. Floods during 1751 brought extreme suffering and recurred the following spring. Reinosa was moved in its entirety to a new site. Revilla was moved three times between 1750 and 1754 before it was sited at the location where it now stands partially buried beneath the waters of the Falcón Reservoir.

When the town locations were ultimately finalized at positions near the river, better planning layouts consistent with old precedents were decreed. On the third of August, 1767, Señor Palacio, Knight of the Order of Saint James, began laying out the towns of Mier, Camargo, and Reinosa.[9] The royal instructions for town planning promulgated in the sixteenth century and utilized in the centuries that followed defined aesthetic and functional qualities that contribute to the delights of many present-day Mexican towns.

Figure 12 shows the locations of Camargo, Mier, and Revilla (that is, Guerrero Viejo.) The boundaries of the Falcón Reservoir—though variable—are indicated in relation to the submerged ranch sites that existed near the former bed of the river. Although ranching and town sites on both sides of the Rio Grande are similar, my *Historic Architecture of Texas: The Falcón Reservoir* included only buildings related to those Texas sites described in the field notes of archaeologist Joe Cason. The communities of Ramireño, Uribeño, San Bartolo, Capitaneño, San Rafaél, Tepezán, La Lajita, Clareño, Lopeño, El Tigre, and Falcón are described in chapter 5 of the current book. And the epilogue includes a photographic essay of Revilla/Guerrero Viejo in the Mexican state of Tamaulipas, which was also partially inundated when the reservoir filled in 1953.

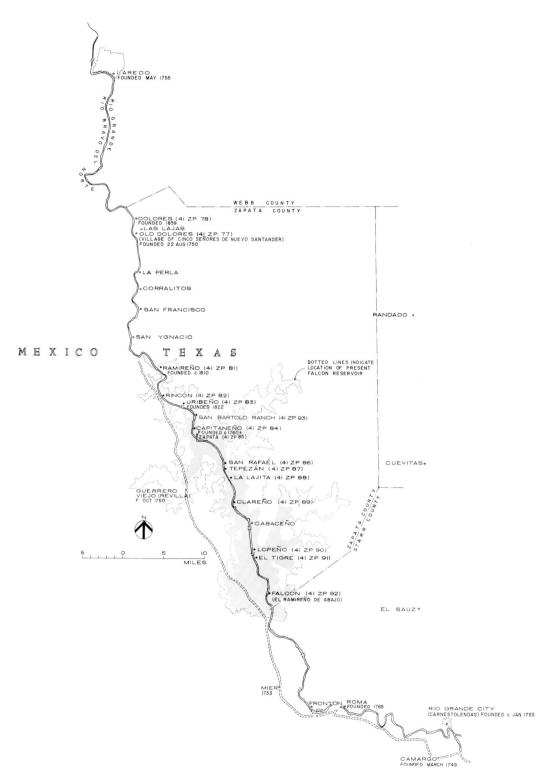

**12.** Map, drawn by author, of Spanish colonial sites within the boundaries of the Falcón Reservoir.

Immigrants moving northward toward the river sites carried seeds that, nourished in virgin soil, would perpetuate that eternal trinity of Mexican agriculture: corn, squash, and beans. Other produce such as pumpkins, peppers, melons, even sugar cane and cotton, if not carried as part of original stocks, would soon be introduced. Though native *carrizal* grasses might have provided material for roof thatching, there are well-founded reports of *tule* being transported from central Mexico to be planted adjacent to the river in the easily irrigated terraces, or *tinajas* (a pool of water trapped in a natural depression above the level of the river.) Also carried in the baggage might be a favorite ornamental to grace the doorway, such as the *flor de mimbres*, or desert willow (*Chilopsis linearis*), which was easily transported over the long, dry distance and whose lavender flowers were a Mexican favorite.

Colonial archaeological middens in the reservoir area reveal that the vegetable diet was supplemented with beef, mutton, and cabrito (roast goat). Meat was often prepared by slicing it into thin, lean strips, then placing the strips on racks to dry in the sun. Called "jerky" or *carne seca,* it was often eaten raw without further preparation. Dried properly, *carne seca* will maintain its vigor for long periods. It can be roasted or form the basis for a stew supplemented with onions, red peppers, potatoes, or other ingredients. Inventories prepared by Tienda de Cuervo during 1757 list large quantities per capita of sheep, goats, and cattle, but especially breeding horses, mules, and asses. An immigration agent wrote: "It will cost more to raise a brood of chickens in Texas than an equal number of cattle." Father Vicente praised "the most beautiful and abundant *grama* grass, which fattens animals until it makes them extraordinarily corpulent, and in every way superior to those of other countries."[10] The colonial immigrants had assembled in a country eminently suitable for grazing. During the Tienda de Cuervo *ynspección* of 1757, the inhabitants stated that they could subsist solely by the stock that they raised and that "if lands should be given them sufficient to extend the breeding of their Stock, [they are] certain they could maintain themselves, because of the great amount of traffic they have in them, some selling them here, and others taking them to other parts."[11] At the time of this inspection, Mier had approximately "400 inhabitants, 38,659 sheep and goats, 3,760 cattle and horses, and 600 tamed beasts." The settlement at Dolores, just north of present-day San Ygnacio, with only twenty-three families could count 400 horses, 3,000 mares, 1,600 mules, and 3,000 cattle.[12]

For protection against Indian raiders, Spanish colonial ranchers encouraged their cattle to run wild. Livestock was handled roughly in order to maintain their feral instincts. And there was a preference for the color black. J. Frank Dobie mentions that milk from a black cow was deemed superior to that of any other—especially for ailing children. Color was also a consideration for horses. In ranging animals, herds were identified by maintaining colors in common, and each *manada* (herd) was carefully separated to prevent intermixing. Horses were a valuable commodity, and ready markets existed in several places.[13] Another important ranching activity was the raising of asses, much in demand by the *arriero* or mule drover for use as pack mules, an occupation initiated early on by the traffic in silver ore and salt. From its beginning, the entire colony was engaged in commerce and trading of salt, beef, mutton, hides, and tallow—exchanging the products of the land for articles required at the ranches. Trade initiated during the eighteenth century would build great fortunes in the nineteenth century.

As herds of horses increased, however, so did incursions by Indians from the north and west. Raiders attacked Falcón in 1790 and in "1792, the colonists suffered frequent invasions from the Apaches, Comanches, Mescaleros, and Kickapoos, especially along the Rio Grande, and as late as 1875, some of these Indians depredated in the Texas border countries."[14] Mexico's 1810 revolt against Spain further threatened the colonists' welfare. On the twenty-ninth of March, 1813, the Spanish units in Texas were defeated and all frontier protection was withdrawn. This was an open invitation to the marauding Indians, who immediately commenced devastating raids on the ranches. Additional raids in 1815 resulted in the abandonment of many ranches north of the river. A family named Ramirez left in such haste "*que nada se sacó de la casa, ni de los muchos bienes de campo que habia*" (that nothing was taken from the house nor from the extensive herds on the range).[15]

Ambrosio de Letinez, a fictitious hero of the early nineteenth century, accurately described the typical architecture of northern Mexico: "The style of building is the Morisco . . . throughout . . . Mexico; that is to say, the houses are almost universally one story high, with flat terrace roofs and few windows to the street. They are frequently built in the form of a quadrangle, round a small courtyard, decorated with evergreens and a fountain, or a little purling stream—a refinement borrowed by modern Mexicans from their Andalusian conquerors. The houses of the poor, however, are nothing but miserable hovels, built of reeds and plastered with clay."[1]

The inspections of 1757 by de Cuervo mentioned houses of hay, more commonly called *jacales*. The hut known as the jacal may consist of various materials and may be carried to different stages of completion.[2] A single room was often constructed of a fence of closely spaced vertical palisades or pickets placed in a continuous trench, thence termed *palisado*. Adobe plaster would then be spread on the inner and outer surfaces, resulting in a tight, substantial wall. A rough framework of wood, often nothing more than the limbs and branches of trees, served as the support for a grass cover of thatch or *tule*. The thatched roof was universal but there were several variations of the vertical exterior walls. Adobe plaster could be omitted, exposing the palisades—the palisades might be spaced to serve as posts with no enclosing wall—or the palisades could be separated to permit a screening partition of horizontal wood members composed of interwoven twigs, branches, split wood, or even bundles of grass.

Walls of adobe brick were mentioned early on, some adjacent to the reservoir area having served to the present time. Roofs sheltering a space enclosed by adobe walls might have two variations: thatch like that used as cover for *jacales,* or flat roofs constructed of horizontal beams (vigas), which were most often covered with thick wooden planks and surfaced with a layer of clay. Structures with stone walls and thatched roofs were also built during the earliest period, often serving as the first "permanent" structure following brief residence in a jacal.[3]

Although vegetal roofs offer superb insulation against heat, flammable thatched roofs proved hazardous to occupants, because the Indians often used fire as an offensive weapon. In order to provide safer quarters for both man and beast when under siege, it was expedient to develop a new type of building: a fortified, windowless stone structure, flat-roofed with a defensive parapet around the perimeter of the roof. The smooth, plastered walls were high enough to deter scaling by a mounted

**13.**
Typical jacal
structure in
Tamaulipas,
Mexico.
Photograph
by Marsha
Jackson,
1970s.

**14.** Stone structure, thatched roof; Vallecillo, Nuevo Leon, Mexico. Photograph by Alex D.
Krieger, January 1953 (Fr 13, 35-mm neg), TARL catalog reference Mexico/Nuevo Leon/Falcón
Reservoir General (8). (For information about Vallecillo, see n3, chap. 3.)

attacker. The exposed surface of the roof was covered with a thick layer of lime concrete, rendering all exterior surfaces, other than doors, fire resistant. *Troneras* (loopholes) embracing a controlled field of fire from weapons within and careful clearing of plant material near the building were other security measures. Local sources mention that after the fortified, flat-roofed structure became common, it would be the first structure to be built in a new settlement. It was often situated on high ground to permit lookouts on the roof to view the surrounding terrain.

Another type of structure, of which few examples are known in the Falcón vicinity, was the *torreón*—a fortified, circular stone tower of two or more stories erected to defend its occupants during attack. A *torreón* had been constructed at Dolores to resist attacks such as those that occurred after 1813, but it was, prudently, never used.[4] Similar *torreones* in New Mexico often proved to be funeral pyres for occupants trapped within their walls.[5]

A pitched-roof stone structure covered originally with thatch but later having a roof of wood shingles imported via river streamer was an additional building type, generally constructed after 1840. End walls were carried above the roof line at the gable forming a low parapet. The tradition continues today in Tamaulipas near the reservoir, where concrete masonry examples are known, roofed either with thatch or corrugated sheet metal.

Most structures located in the reservoir basin were randomly placed on the site and not joined together to form a court, nor were they surrounded by high outer defensive walls. There were, however, instances of defensive walls surrounding entire groups of buildings. Expansion of the original one-room units was achieved either by adding a similar room in alignment lengthwise with the original unit, or by the addition of shed rooms of palisadoed construction, stone, or wooden planks in the form of a "lean-to" against the original structure. Expansion was often preplanned with projecting stones at the corners to ensure good bonding for the add-on unit. Proportions of floor plans, door openings, end walls, and other elements are so well handled as to suggest the knowledge of geometric commensurability, certainly known by designers of eighteenth-century Franciscan churches.

The ochre-colored sandstone, so easily quarried along the banks of that stretch of the Rio Grande, was a primary building material in the Escandón settlements. The quality of the stone masonry attested to a knowledge of masonry techniques from the earliest settlements. Corners of walls and door openings were formed with carefully squared and dressed stones laid up with narrow joints, while the wall stones were roughly trimmed quarry blocks with outer faces trued to alignment. Stone walls were bonded with adobe mud or lime mortar. Small horizontal stones, sometimes forming an overall wall pattern, were often inserted into the joints—a somewhat crude manifestation of the patterned central Mexican stonework known as *rejoneado*. Such thin stones assist bonding strength of an exterior surface of plaster coating applied to a masonry wall. The rough stone portions of the wall were

**15.** Stone structure, thatched roof, detail of fence construction; Vallecillo, Nuevo Leon, Mexico. Photograph by Alex D. Krieger, January 1953 (Fr 7, 35-mm, third excavation), TARL catalog reference Mexico/Nuevo Leon/Falcón Reservoir General (2).

**16.**
Loophole
(*tronera*) from
interior; Dolores
Viejo, Zapata
County, Texas.
Photograph by
Marsha Jackson,
ca. 1970s.

**17.**
Loophole
(*tronera*)
from interior;
Capitaneño,
Zapata
County, Texas.
Photograph by
Alex D. Krieger,
January 1953
(Steen no. 328;
no negative),
TARL catalog
reference
41ZP84 (1).

**18.** House (circa 1810); Ramireño, Zapata County, Texas.
Photograph by Bob Humphreys, 1950 (2x2 neg), TARL catalog reference 41ZP81 (3).

frequently coated with a thin layer of lime stucco, leaving the quoins at the corners as well as the trim surrounding the doorway exposed. Interior walls were plastered with the same material. Carved stone moldings, rain heads, door arches, and projecting rain spouts or *canales* are known on the Mexican side of the river, but few examples are found associated with Texas buildings. A detail of interest with examples in the reservoir area was round buttresses located at the corners of exterior walls of several of the buildings, known as a bollaster or *contrafuerte*. This device may have protected fragile corners from cart wheel hubs, or it may have served to stabilize corner thrusts by masonry walls that were weakly cemented with mud mortar.

Lime as a constituent for mortar and plaster was locally manufactured. Maj. W. E. Emory, in his mid-nineteenth-century survey, mentioned reefs of gigantic shellfish exposed as fossils along the river, and oyster shells as large as twenty-four inches in diameter have been found nearby in Starr County. During archaeological investigation, Cason noted heavy concentrations of marl in association with a third of the area sites. Fossilized oyster shells provided a principal component for the manufacture of lime (cal). Other lime-bearing materials, including marl and caliche, are said to have been used. Kiln sites for burning lime, identified in the course of archaeological inquiry, were located in banks of arroyos above the river. In the 1850 census, a tragic story was mentioned. Guadalupe Cordova, his wife, María, and their son,

**19.** Stone wall, built by typical Mexican masonry technique known as *rejoneado;* Revilla (Guerrero Viejo), Tamaulipas, Mexico. José Guerrero stands beside wall of "Old Fort" (*left*) and more recent construction (*center*). Photograph by Alex D. Krieger, July 1950 (Fr 33, 35-mm neg), TARL catalog reference Mexico/Tamaulipas/Falcón Reservoir General (8).

José, were blinded by burning lime, surely an accident caused by unsafe slaking procedures.[6]

Major Emory also observed that "above Roma to the mouth of the Salado and up the Salado there is an abundance of cypress along the shores." Peñitas, downstream, had served as a lumber camp since the earliest Spanish intrusions northward.[7] Krieger and Hughes reported that the Spaniards, early on, noted the absence of oaks in the lower Rio Grande valley and for some distance on either side of it.[8] On the other hand, Father Vicente inventoried "the variety of woods [such as] ebony, cedar, box-wood, and other kinds of no small value in the colony and along the coast of the Seno Mexico."[9]

Cypress and mesquite were the natural construction woods obtainable in the locale of the Escandón settlements and are the only types of timber to be used until 1850 when steamboats began carrying upstream cargoes of northern softwoods.[10] Straight and long, Montezuma bald cypress (*Taxodium mucronatum*) was the desired choice for lumber, that is timber that can be sawed or split into planks or boards. This species, though abundant along the banks of the Salado, the Sabinas, and portions of the Rio Grande, has its northern limit at the Rio Grande; the boundary of its southern growth extends southward deep into Mexico. Known as *huehuetl* by the Aztecs and as *ahuehuete* by the early Spaniards, it is rooted in significant portions of Spanish colonial history. Cypress is easily worked, durable, and long lasting. The mesquite that was often used as a construction material in the study area

**20.** Lime kiln (archaeological feature, remnant of base); Gutierrez, Zapata County, Texas. Photograph attributed to Joe Cason, 1952 (3x5 negative; TARL print reversed), TARL catalog reference 41ZP63 (1).

is the Torrey mesquite (*Prosopis juliflora var. torreyana*), a local tree not to be confused with the more commonly known honey mesquite. It is durable when properly seasoned. Though the figure and grain of polished mesquite will delight the most discriminating connoisseur, it is very hard to work because of its tough, irregular grain. Mesquite was employed for lintels above door openings and fireplaces, and also for doorjambs and thresholds. Wooden thresholds were used when doors were operated on pivots. They were often large in cross section—as much as five by seven inches—and were drilled near the jamb to receive the pivot extending down from the jamb stile (*montante quicial*). Mesquite is also an excellent firewood and burns with a white heat.

For drainage, seemingly flat roofs had a modest, almost imperceptible slope. Roof beams, commonly called vigas, were generally square-hewn cypress, though mesquite was also used. Vigas varied in cross-sectional dimensions from four to eight to as much as twelve by twelve inches. Determined by the nature of the material resting on their upper surfaces, vigas were spaced at narrow intervals. Round poles with an upper flattened surface were also used. Corbels or *ejiones,* wedge-shaped short blocks of wood, often carved, were placed in the masonry during wall construction, with their top surfaces projecting into the interior space and aligned to cradle the bottoms of the vigas.

Decorated vigas—carved with religious or patriotic inscriptions as well as painted symbolic motifs—were often found but restricted to one centered in each room. Inscriptions were usually on the soffits of the vigas, and the two lower corners of inscribed beams were often chamfered or beaded (*bordón*). Thick cypress planks of random width known as *tablas* often spanned the vigas to form a deck for the roof. The same purpose was served by cane coverings as well as small pieces of wood known as *latias*. Often *latias* are described by the species of wood used, that is, *cedros* (cedar), *savinos* (cypress), or even *rajas* (splits).

A leveling layer of earth with a thickness of three to four inches would be laid on top of the *tablas,* and on top of this would be placed an outer exposed cover of lime concrete containing a pea-gravel aggregate (*chipichil* or *tipichil*). The lime concrete cover would be two or more inches thick and sloped to drain toward the *canales.* *Canales,* U-shaped wooden or stone gutters, penetrated the roof parapet to carry the runoff water well clear of the wall to the ground.

Jacal roofs were constructed over a framework of poles or branches. Natural projections such as twigs, joints, natural crooks, or forks were arranged to interlock, as well as to serve as a lashing place where twine or rawhide ties could secure them together.

Pitched roofs in all cases employed a substantial ridge pole from gable to gable, with rafters secured from the ridge to a plate securely resting on a massive stone wall. Ceiling joists were not employed since thrust was adequately resisted by the ridge in combination with the mass of masonry. Rafters were covered by solid *tablas* or by nailing strips to provide attachment for the outer covering of thatch or shingles. A most pleasant space resulted from this type of construction. Wherever possible, rainwater was collected and diverted to a cistern or well. In most of the examples studied, structures from the earliest period had suffered through periods of incongruous modification. Finding a 1910 period hipped roof on an 1840 fortified house was not uncommon.

Doors, either singly or in pairs, were substantial, with heavy mortised and pegged frames of mesquite, rabbeted to receive wide cypress panels. Elements of joinery were artistically detailed, including bevels, slight curves, and other simple devices. Windows were unknown on the ranches during the early period, though small grilled openings made of wood often provided ventilation. Wooden shelves for storage were common, often placed on wooden or stone brackets set into the masonry wall during construction. Shelves were most often positioned above door openings, though shelves at head height were also located on interior walls. Shallow niches recessed into stone walls were also common storage elements, though generally only one per room. Niches were placed high on the wall beyond the reach of children. Often in the vicinity of the fireplace wall along one of the side walls was a *banqueta,* a continuous bench of masonry on which one might sit, place utensils, or even prepare a narrow bed. Descriptions of Spanish colonial crafts related to the provinces of New Mexico and Texas often apologize for the poor quality of wood craftsmanship relating to building and the decorative arts. In the focus area of this study, stone masonry of good quality was evident almost from the first founding.

**21.** Flat roof construction showing lime concrete slab (*chipichil*) at top of roof. Photograph attributed to Edward B. Jelks, TARL catalog reference 41ZP Falcón General (C22) (color slide, site not identified).

**22.** Pitched roof construction; Vallecillo, Nuevo Leon, Mexico. Photograph by Alex D. Krieger, January 1953 (Fr 10, 35-mm neg), TARL catalog reference Mexico/Nuevo Leon/Falcón Reservoir General (7).

**23.** Jacal roof, detail of Figure 22; Vallecillo, Nuevo Leon, Mexico. Photograph by Alex D. Krieger, January 1953 (Fr 11, 35-mm neg), TARL catalog reference Mexico/Nuevo Leon/Falcón Reservoir General (10).

**24.** Pitched roof showing ridge construction; Vallecillo, Nuevo Leon, Mexico. Photograph by Alex D. Krieger, January 1953 (Fr 14, 35-mm neg), TARL catalog reference Mexico/Nuevo Leon/ Falcón Reservoir General (6).

Evidence that talent in the building arts was being encouraged downriver at Mier is provided by de Cuervo in his 1757 report. He mentioned that among the neophytes "one had become a stonemason, one a blacksmith, and two had learned the carpenter's trade."[11]

Early on, furnishings of wood were manufactured locally, including free-standing cupboards (*trasteros*), chests, tables, benches, and beds. Carpentry craftsmanship of the pre-1850 period, as observed in examples near the reservoir, is very good. (See the drawings by Jorge Pardo in the introduction.)

Massive fireplaces made of stone surfaced with lime plaster were often an integral part of the structure. A fireplace might be located against a lateral wall near a corner with the chimney and firebox on the exterior. Usually, however, it would be similarly positioned on an end wall. Free-standing fireplace units, placed adjacent to an interior wall or corner, are additions to the original construction. Fireplaces were also constructed as part of shed rooms added to earlier units. Exterior fireplaces for cooking served outside covered spaces known as *ramadas* (generally a brush-roofed arbor) or *galerías* (arcades). Recesses in the massive free-standing fireplaces provided storage adjacent to areas of food preparation. The *horno,* an oven especially for baking, was a hollow hemisphere of stone, smoothly plastered on the exterior and six to eight feet in diameter, which rested on an elevated, square stone base. Abandoned

**25.** Pitched roof, construction from interior; San Bartolo, Zapata County, Texas. Photograph by Bob Humphreys, summer 1950 (2x2 neg), TARL catalog reference 41ZP93 (3).

**26.** House 2, mesquite window grille (*reja*); Uribeño, Zapata County, Texas.
Photograph attributed to Edward B. Jelks (Fr 36. 35-mm neg), TARL catalog reference 41ZP83 (2).

*hornos* now serve as shelter for chickens, dogs, and rattlesnakes. Fragments of cooking and serving vessels such as iron pots and stake-formed copper vessels have been found among the site debris. Archaeological inquiry has identified pottery shards of majolica, mocha ware, "gaudy Dutch," and "gaudy Staffordshire" hand-painted earthenware, transfer-printed earthenware bearing English manufacturer's marks, and even Chinese porcelain.

Because floors were often sunk slightly below ground level outside, one entered downward over the threshold into the interior, which contributed to a secure feeling of spatial enclosure. Clay, flagstone (*lajas*), or lime concrete (*chipichil*) were customary floor surfaces. Neither tile—generally associated with Mexican buildings—nor adobe were used in the documented examples. Animal blood as a surface hardener for clay floors may have been used, since it was known to have been used in Texas, but no evidence of this technique was revealed in the buildings soon to be submerged beneath the water of the reservoir.

Illumination was provided, initially, by the fireplace and by candles. After marauding Indians departed from the frontier in the late 1870s, windows were cut into the walls to beneficial effect. Kerosene lamps were introduced after 1870, and were still being used in 1961 at the time of my initial borderlands investigations. Interior

**27.** Baking oven (*horno*); Lopeño, Zapata County, Texas.
Photograph by Jack Hughes, 1950 (4x5 neg), TARL catalog reference 41ZP90 (5).

walls were whitewashed to reduce interior gloom caused by the windowless space and to discourage insects.

Iron hardware was used on buildings, cupboards, and chests and some had brass working parts and handles. A hinge or *gozne* often consisted of interlocking eye-rings with protruding, split shanks that passed through a drilled hole and clinched. Modified butterfly hinges of iron, wood, and the ubiquitous rawhide were also used. Doors were sometimes secured on the interior by a unique Spanish form of self-locking hasp, which was further strengthened by a bar of wood. Padlocks were also found during the archaeological inquiry.

One hundred years after the founding of the Escandón settlements—a century of dire calamities—dangers were mitigated and the economy was improving. The built environment offered evidence that, by the mid-nineteenth century, life in the borderlands could be pleasant for descendants of those valiant early pioneers, at least the affluent. After 1850, furniture and other luxury goods from eastern, midwestern, and even European sources arrived through the port of New Orleans and were transshipped by steamboat up the Rio Grande to Roma for distribution throughout the territory. Colorful fragments of pottery bespeak an existence that was far from dreary. Other evidence included painted geometric or floral decorations around the principal entrance of a building, as well as painted architectural allusions: pilasters with capitals, simulated bands of moldings, entablatures, and other references to elegance. And as is evident in the photographic essay in the epilogue, there were far more than mere painted architectural allusions in Revilla/Guerrero Viejo.

A traveler's journal, a report of a military reconnaissance, and an author's fictional account all describe borderlands buildings and their contents. And all were written around the middle of the nineteenth century. Although none specifically refer to the area later submerged beneath the waters of the Falcón Reservoir, all are consistent with contemporaneous evidence.

An 1838 description of a domestic household along the Rio Grande appears in *The First Texian Novel* and evokes delightful imagery:

> It was a little cabin, built of large unburnt bricks, called adobes, in the language of the country, and thatched with *tule,* a kind of rush that grows in the swampy bottoms of the Rio Bravo, and are nearly incombustible. The thatch itself, by the effects of time, has been reduced to an earthy mass, now shrunk into consistency, and affording sustenance to a multiplicity of parasitic plants, which, being in full bloom, gave it the appearance of a parterre. Among them, various kinds of cacti, and young mimosas were remarkable, some with pink blossoms, and others with pale yellow ones. . . . The furniture consisted of a little cot, with coarse, though extremely clean bed clothes, a small table, four old chairs without backs, and a mattress rolled up in a corner, which being spread at night on a rug carpet, served one of the inmates for a bed. Some crockery ware upon a shelf, a few books on the mantel-piece, and two trunks completed the inventory. . . . [The master of the house] was culling fruit in the *huerta* [vegetable garden] and immediately opened a side door made of wattled reeds, giving access to a little courtyard. . . . It was rather a kind of orchard, full of fig, pomegranate and orange trees, planted without attention to symmetry. They were so thick and their foliage was so dense, as to afford a coolness extremely pleasant in that southern climate; and moreover produced a kind of artificial night upon the vision of one, who coming from the glare of the broad day-light, entered this deep shade.[1]

Major W. H. Emory encountered domestic interiors in the course of an 1846 military reconnaissance far upstream from the reservoir area at another *villa* on the Rio Grande just north of Albuquerque. Though the differences between settlements in Texas and those in New Mexico are great, similarities warrant their consideration as variants of the same culture. This is confirmed by the following description:

The town of Bernalillo is small, but one of the best built in the territory. We were invited to the house of a wealthy man to take refreshment . . . and were led into an oblong room, furnished like that of every other Mexican in comfortable circumstances. A banquette runs around the room, leaving only a space for the couch. It is covered with cushions, carpets, and pillows upon which the visitor sits or reclines. The dirt floor is usually covered a third or a half with common looking carpet. On the uncovered part is the table, freighted with grapes, sponge-cake, and the wine of the country. The walls are hung with miserable pictures of the saints, crosses innumerable, and Yankee mirrors without number. These last are suspended entirely out of reach; and if one wishes to shave or adjust his toilet, he must do so without the aid of a mirror, be there ever so many in the chamber. . . . It was a queer jumble of refinement and barbarism. . . . The plates, forks, and spoons were of solid New Mexican silver, clumsily worked in the country. . . . At close intervals were glass decanters of Pittsburgh manufacture, filled with wine made on the plantation.[2]

Frederick Law Olmsted, later celebrated as the father of American landscape architecture, was traveling by horseback through Texas in the spring of 1854 and crossed the Rio Grande to visit the Mexican *villa* of San Fernando. The early, flat-roofed buildings like those found within the area of the Falcón reservoir are delineated in his descriptions:

The houses were . . . generally of a superior character, many of them being built of stone and most of them plastered over and whitewashed. Some were ornamented with bright colored stripes about their doors . . . with stenciled leaves and rosettes. The doors, window cages, and roof spouts were much carved, often with representations in relief, facetiously rude of course, of men and angels and birds and beasts. . . . Outside [a particular dwelling], the house appeared a mere plain, dead wall of adobes, having except the single door of the entrance, no other openings than the spout-holes of the roof. Within, was a single room, about forty feet long and fifteen broad, the floor of hard-trodden earth, and the ceiling some sixteen feet above it, of bamboo, laid with cement, on small, crooked, unhewn rafters. As there were no windows, and but two small, low doors, there was a great depth of gloom overhead. At one end, upon the whitewashed wall, hung a large old painting, the subject imperceptible except to the eye of faith: a crucifix over it: a small painting of a mermaid-like martyr, with long draggling, unsinged hair, rising, head and shoulders, out of a sea of fire; and several coarse woodcuts of saints and friars. Near this, on a narrow shelf, was a blunderbuss, a horse-pistol, and a thin prayer-book, the only literature in the house. At this end of the room were three broad beds, with elaborately worked cover-lids, used in the day as lounges. Two large chests . . . stood next to the beds, then a sort of settle, or high-backed bench, against the wall, wide enough to be used for a bed:

then a broad, low table, used for a dining table when any one dined in the house, also as a bedstead for two at night. A little box or crib, in which a baby lay sucking its fists, swung near the floor by a hide rope from the ceiling. . . . Somewhat to my consternation, I found that the señor was leading my horse in at the door. The horse followed him readily enough, no doubt thinking it a stable, and feeling fully as much at home as I did. . . . Near the end opposite to that I have described, was a back door; out of this, presently, they went out, our host and the pony, the others following. This end of the house had no other furniture than a cupboard and a few forms, on which were calabashes and earthen pots. A saddle or two, also, hung here, and some fowls were picking about. The door opened upon a house-court and garden, which was enclosed by high and strong palisades. . . . The horses . . . were rolling on the smooth ground of the courtyard, and drinking from the acequia which divided it from the garden. In this courtyard were several walnut and fig trees, under which our horses were fastened; also, a high dome-formed oven, made of adobes, one of which is to be seen behind every Mexican house, though I nowhere saw one in use, except for a chicken-coop or dog-kennel. Various vegetables were growing in the garden, but more maize than all else. Hearing a continual slap, slap, slap in the next yard, I looked between the stakes to see what made the sound. A woman . . . was kneeling upon the ground, under a fig-tree close to the fence, rubbing the *matate,* and a pretty girl of fifteen was kneeling before her, clapping her hands, or rather slapping a tortilla between them. . . . A fire was made upon the ground in a corner of the yard near the door of the house, one woman went to hashing a haunch of kid, another sliced some onions, leeks, and red peppers.[3]

Life along the Rio Grande could indeed be pleasant for descendants of those valiant early pioneers. Beginning in the early nineteenth century, however, waves of political, social, and cultural disorganization swept through the borderlands and eroded the centuries-old class structure of Mexican ranch settlements. These changes are documented by David Montejano and Andrés Tijerina.[4] While these traumatic events are beyond the scope of this book, a brief consideration of the factors that stabilized and strengthened this culture for many decades is appropriate—beset by all manner of dangers and hardships as it was.

In the Mexican ranch settlements of the border region, the preservation of a traditional lifestyle whose roots and traditions dated back to Spanish colonization in the mid-eighteenth century was of primary importance. Shared interests, shared worldviews, personal faith and a conception of what was proper and just held ranch society together.[5] Parents took the necessary steps to attain this end and gave their children a Mexican education. "The wealthy sent their children to the schools in Mexico, principally Monterrey and Saltillo, those in moderate circumstances sent theirs to private Mexican schools in Texas, while the children of the servant class did not attend school at all. In fact the landowners discouraged the working class getting an education on the ground that this would ruin them for the work they had to do." So wrote Jovita González based on interviews with long-time residents of the area who were keepers of shared memories handed down through the generations.[6]

Emilia Schunior Ramírez wrote the following description of the priest's visit to isolated borderlands settlements:

> Nearly all of the settlers on the ranches were Catholic, but prior to 1900 there were very few missionaries. Oblate Fathers, with headquarters at Brownsville or Rio Grande [City] or Roma, and much later, La Lomita, visited the ranches as often as they could, but travel by horseback was slow, and the ranches were scattered over a large area. The mothers and aunts took the responsibility for teaching the children the Christian catechism, but no sacraments could be administered until the priest came. For that reason, the coming of the priest was always an occasion of great significance. All the unbaptized babies were christened. Mass was celebrated. Confessions were heard and Holy Communion was received. Weddings were solemnized. The spiritual life of the community was revived; the blessing of the Lord was more keenly felt with the presence of the spiritual advisor. Weddings and baptisms were celebrated with the greatest elaborateness. There was always an abundance of food, and at weddings at least there was music and gaiety. There were special foods served on these occasions, and they were always served to all the guests in plentiful quantities. A wedding might last all night and all the following day. Some weddings lasted three days.[7]

The French-born Joseph Marie Closs was one of the oblate priests who rode through the wilderness of the border country. In the mid-nineteenth century, he was sent as a missionary priest to the lower Rio Grande region. There for fifty years he was priest, physician, and adviser to his parishioners—"his spiritual children in every sense of the word. He baptized, married, and buried them. He laughed with the happy, wept with the sad, comforted them in their vicissitudes and ministered to them in their sickness. He was a picturesque figure as he rode through the border country on his white horse, wearing deerskin leggings and a broad-brimmed hat tied under the chin. Because of his ability as a rider, he was known as the cowboy priest."[8]

Another oblate priest, Pierre Yves Keralum (1817–72), arrived from France in 1852 and would ride the extended missionary circuits from ranch to ranch over the vast territories of South Texas for two decades where he was revered as "El Santo Padre Pedrito."[9] In addition to his spiritual devotion, Father Keralum brought needed skills, manifestations of which survive to the present. (See the description of his architectural legacy at the end of this chapter.)

Following the completion of his secondary education in France, Keralum became a cabinetmaker, later studying architecture in Paris. Following his success as an architectural practitioner, he made his profession as an oblate of Mary Immaculate and was ordained in 1852 at age thirty-five. His parish extended upriver from Brownsville, where his dedication soon became known. It was said he would rush to a remote location to be at the bedside of a failing parishioner, administer last rites, spend much of the night employing his cabinetmaker skills preparing a proper coffin, then observe Requiem on the following morning.

Because of the mysterious circumstances of Father Keralum's death, he is also remembered as "the Lost Missionary." At age fifty-six and almost blind, he began a routine circuit ride, departing Brownsville on November 9, 1872. (The strenuous life he led along the Rio Grande, including many personal privations, had caused him to age prematurely.) Three days later, he arrived at Tampacuas Ranch, four miles north of Mercedes as scheduled. From there, he departed for the ranch of Las Piedras some eighteen miles northward. He never reached his destination. His horse was discovered unfettered but dragging a lariat. Immediately search parties were assembled but no trace of the beloved priest was found. Much speculation and rumor surrounded his disappearance. Requiem high mass was celebrated in his honor at Brownsville three months later. Ten years later, in 1882, a rancher went into thick chaparral to disentangle two cows. There he found the skeletal remains of Father Keralum, identified by his oblate cross, the chalice and paten, a holy oil stock, altar bread box, a holy water bottle, a piece of rosary, an altar bell, a watch, and eighteen dollars in silver. His saddle was carefully hung on a tree and none of his belongings were missing so that it was thought he died of illness or was attacked by wild animals.

Paul Horgan published a fictional account based on the vicissitudes of Father Keralum's life that describes an encounter between a serpent and the priest in his final hours. The author's evocation of "coyotes and blowing sands, vultures and beating sunlight and wind"—though fictional are quite believable.[10] Surely the spiritual sustenance offered by the circuit-riding missionary priests instilled the will to survive in the stalwart pioneers of the Rio Grande borderlands.

### THE ARCHITECTURAL LEGACY OF PIERRE YVES KERALUM, O.M.I.

IN ROMA, **Starr County. Our Lady of Refuge of Sinners.** Father Keralum served not only as priest and architect for the church but also as stonecutter and mason. The cornerstone was laid September 18, 1854. The landmark church crowning the plaza was destroyed, except the tower, and was replaced "in the name of progress" by a modern air-conditioned church that was dedicated in 1965. In 1961, I documented the Keralum-designed building for the Historic American Buildings Survey. Photo Data book TEX 3135.

IN BROWNSVILLE, **Cameron County, Church of the Immaculate Conception.** After the oblate superior who had been supervising the building of the church drowned at sea, Keralum was entrusted with modifying the plans and seeing the building through to completion. Parishioners made by hand the needed 250,000 bricks from local clay. The Brownsville church, which was completed in 1859, was designated a cathedral in 1874.

IN LAREDO, **Webb County, San Agustín de Laredo.** In the summer of 1872, the year of his death, Keralum assisted the diocesan priests who were building the new church, also later a cathedral, of San Agustín on the plaza in Laredo. Following the design of an earlier colonial-period church; the present church was blessed on December 22, 1872. It was probably designed by Pierre Keralum for the secular priests in Laredo as it had earlier been an oblate responsibility.

IN SANTA MARIA in western Cameron County, **Church of Our Lady of Visitation.** Keralum executed preliminary designs before his death in 1872. Completed and blessed in 1880.[11]

Investigation of the valley floor of what was to become the Falcón Reservoir was accomplished in the course of archaeological field surveys begun in 1949 and completed in January 1953. (See appendix for specific details.) Archaeological sites were identified by code designations and named for the ranch or settlement nearest to the position of the investigation. Though Spanish sites located on the Texas side of the Rio Grande were but one of several areas of concentration of the survey, those settlements and ranch sites were the primary focus of my book *Historic Architecture of Texas: The Falcón Reservoir.*

The photographs in this chapter, as well as measurements, rough sketches, archaeological notes, and descriptions in Joe F. Cason's notebooks, provided documentation used in preparing the drawings that accompany the photographs. Unless a north arrow indicates otherwise, the drawings are oriented so that the direction north is toward the top of the page.

**Ramireño:** (41zp81) lat 26°59′38″ N, long 99°23′35″ W. Located five miles southeast of the present town of San Ygnacio on the east side of the Rio Grande channel and north of Arroyo Burro. (See Fig. 28.)

José Luís Ramírez and Basilia Martínez moved to the site and established a settlement in 1810. Manuel Ramírez y Martínez (born Revilla, 1799–died 1882) was captured near the site by Comanches in 1819; he was returned circa 1822 after ransom was paid in Louisiana.

**Rincón:** (41zp82) lat 26°56′30″ N, long 99°23′03″ W. Also called Rancho de Guadalupe. Located on the east side of the Rio Grande channel eight miles south-southeast of the present town of San Ygnacio. Inscription on viga: RANCHO DE GUADALUPE JUNIO 24 DE 1867 SIRVO A SU DUENO VIVIANO GARCIA VIVA LA HORA DE DIOS VIVA LA PAZ

**Uribeño:** (41zp83) lat 26°55′43″ N, long 99°20′24″ W. Located on the east side of the Rio Grande channel ten miles southeast of the present town of San Ygnacio. Site originally selected because of proximity to ford known as El Paso Chaveno, also called Las Corrientes de Golandrinas. Original settlement established in 1822 by Doña Ygnacia (widow of Don Dionisio) Uribe and two sons, Blas María Uribe (born circa 1811–died 1895) and Juan José Uribe (born circa 1813–died ?) In 1830

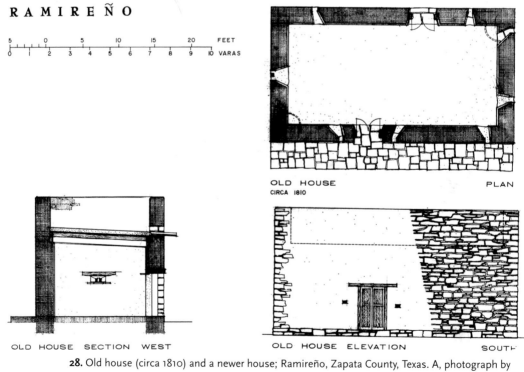

**RAMIREÑO**

OLD HOUSE
CIRCA 1810                          PLAN

OLD HOUSE SECTION WEST

OLD HOUSE ELEVATION          SOUTH

**28.** Old house (circa 1810) and a newer house; Ramireño, Zapata County, Texas. A, photograph by Bob Humphreys, 1950 (2x2 neg), TARL catalog reference 41ZP81 (3); B, the old house, analytical drawings by the author; C, newer house, analytical drawings by the author.

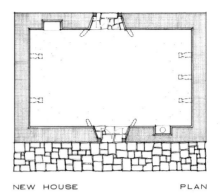

NEW HOUSE                    PLAN

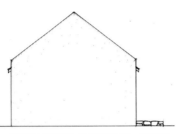

NEW HOUSE ELEVATION WEST

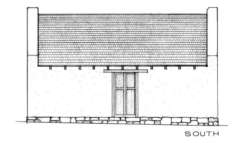

SOUTH

NEW HOUSE SECTION WEST

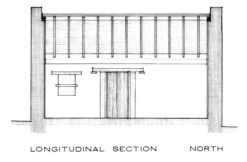

LONGITUDINAL SECTION    NORTH

C

Blas María bought land in San Ygnacio from the heirs of the original grantor (José Vásquez Borrego) and moved to this more settled and hence less hazardous location. (See Fig. 29.)

**San Bartolo:** (41ZP93) lat 26°54′30″ N, long 99°19′14″ W. Located on the east side of the Rio Grande channel eleven and a half miles southeast of the present town of San Ygnacio. Identified by HABS number HABS TEX-3–113. (See Fig. 30.)

**Capitaneño:** (41ZP84) lat 26°53′14″ N, long 99°19′12″ W. Located on the east side of the Rio Grande channel thirteen miles southeast of the present town of San Ygnacio. Fortified flat-roofed stone buildings constructed prior to 1780, possibly as early as 1760 by Captain José Miguel de Cuéllar. Captain Cuéllar originally came from Querétaro to Revilla, thence to Capitaneño. Principal building originally had a second story. According to local tradition, John James Audubon visited this ranch in April 1848 and collected data for his painting of the roadrunner included in *Birds of America.*

**Tepezán:** (41ZP87) lat 26°49′14″ N, long 99°15′21″ W. Located on the east side of the Rio Grande channel twenty miles southeast of the present town of San Ygnacio. Names mentioned in connection with this site are Leal Juárez; Isidro Vela, and his wife, Bernarda Valdéz; Salinas Vela; Santiago Vela; Tomás Vela; and Inocente Peña. (See Fig. 31.)

**San Rafaél:** (41ZP86) lat 26°49′36″ N, long 99°15′21″ W. Located on the east side of the Rio Grande channel nineteen miles southeast of the present town of San Ygnacio.

**Lopeño:** (41ZP90) lat 26°40′46″ N, long 99°12′12″ W. Located on the east side of the Rio Grande channel seven miles north of present Falcón Dam. Proximity to river crossing determined site selection. Lopeño Crossing one half mile south of site. (See Fig. 32.)
Original grant to Ysabel María Sánchez in 1761 passed to the Ramírez family early in the nineteenth century. Don Benito Ramírez built principal structure—residence, fort, and chapel combined—at the south entrance to main village in 1821.

**Falcón:** (41ZP92) lat 26°36′04″ N, long 99°10′17″ W. Located on the east side of the Rio Grande channel one and a half miles north of the present Falcón Dam. Also called El Ramireño del Abajo until 1915. A river ford existed adjacent to the site. (See Fig. 33.)
Original grant to José Clemente Ramírez by *general visita* July 7, 1767. In 1780 title passed to Don José Ramírez, treasurer of the church at Revilla. That same year,

he married Rita de la Garza Falcón, a native of the Congregación del Refugio, now Matamoros. Moved to Falcón soon after marriage and constructed first residence there about 1781.

**La Lajita:** (41ZP88) lat 26°48′10″ N, long 99°15′02″ W. Located on the east side of the Rio Grande channel twenty-one miles southeast of the present-day town of San Ygnacio. It was across the river from the settlement of Revilla/Guerrero Viejo. (See Fig. 34.)

The two-story house on the site was in ruins at the time of the survey. It had a flat roof, walls buttressed by massive circular stone corner elements (*contrafuertes* or bollasters). There were also ruins and foundations of other buildings on the site. Vela was the family name.

**Clareño:** (41ZP89) lat 26°46′04″ N, long 99°14′16″ W. Located on the east side of the Rio Grande channel twenty-three miles southeast of the present town of San Ygnacio. (See Figs. 35 and 36.)

The principal structure was the residence of Isidro Vela, a judge, who was murdered in the house December 26, 1862.

**El Tigre:** (41ZP91) lat 26°39′40″ N, long 99°11′46″ W. Located on the east side of the Rio Grande channel six miles north of the present Falcón Dam. (Not to be confused with El Tigre de Bajo one mile southeast of the site.)

Stone ranch buildings. Feature of interest is the carved stone shrine with a sculpture of Our Lady of Guadalupe, also identified as the Virgin of the Immaculate Conception. The monument was erected above a combination cistern-well by either Don Benito Ramírez or Don Silvestre Ramírez about 1850—glorifying a patron saint and using her effigy to guard the well. (See Fig. 37.)

**29.** House 2; Uribeño, Zapata County, Texas. A, west facade, showing doorway and grille; photograph attributed to Edward B. Jelks (Fr 4, 4x5 neg), TARL catalog reference 41ZP83(3); B, analytical drawings by the author.

A

URIBEÑO

5    0    5    10    15    20   FEET
0  1  2  3  4  5  6  7  8  9  10 VARAS

URIBEÑO HOUSE 2   PLAN

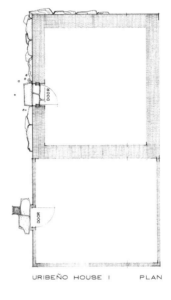

URIBEÑO HOUSE 1    PLAN

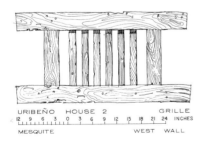

URIBEÑO HOUSE 2    GRILLE
12 9 6 3  0  3 6 9 12 15 18 21 24 INCHES
MESQUITE        WEST WALL

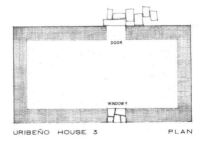

URIBEÑO HOUSE 3      PLAN

B

**30.** House; San Bartolo, Zapata County, Texas. Photograph by Bob Humphreys, summer 1950 (2x2 neg), TARL catalog reference 41ZP93 (5).

A

**31.** Leal Juarez house; Tepezán, Zapata County, Texas. A, view southwest; photograph attributed to Edward B. Jelks (Fr 38, 35-mm neg), TARL catalog reference 41ZP87(1). B, analytical drawings by the author. The man standing to the right is an unidentified member of the archaeological team.

# TEPEZÁN

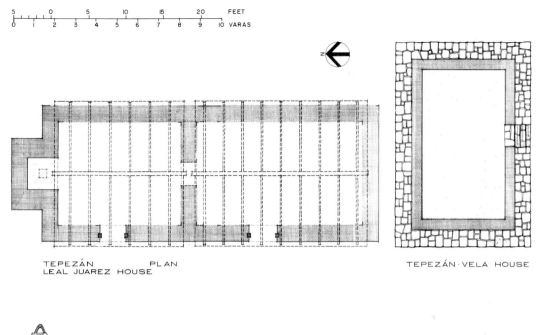

TEPEZÁN · VELA HOUSE

TEPEZÁN      PLAN
LEAL JUAREZ HOUSE

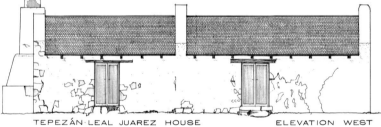

TEPEZÁN·LEAL JUAREZ HOUSE      ELEVATION WEST

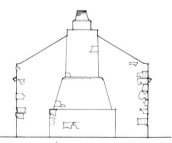

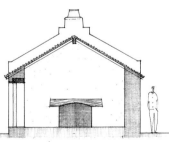

TEPEZÁN·ELEVATION NORTH
LEAL JUAREZ HOUSE

TEPEZÁN·SECTION NORTH
LEAL JUAREZ HOUSE

B

A

**32.** House 2; Lopeño, Zapata County, Texas. A, south facade (with bollasters); photograph by Jack Hughes(?) (Fr 40, 35-mm neg), TARL catalog reference 41ZP90 (1); B, analytical drawings by the author.

# LOPEÑO

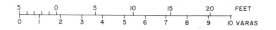

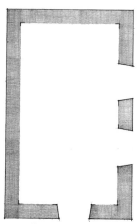

LOPEÑO · HOUSE 1 · PLAN

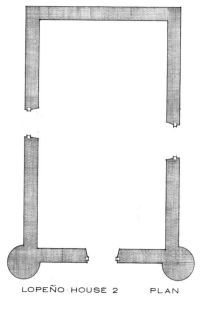

LOPEÑO · HOUSE 2        PLAN

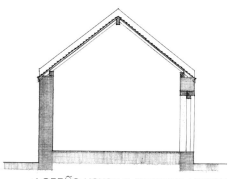

LOPEÑO · HOUSE 2 · ELEVATION · SOUTH

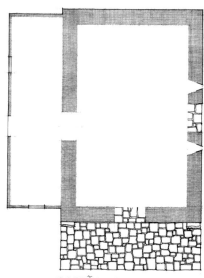

LOPEÑO · HOUSE 3        PLAN

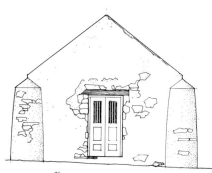

LOPEÑO · HOUSE 2 · SECTION · NORTH

B

A

**33.** House 2; Falcón, Zapata County, Texas. A, view northeast; photograph by Bob Humphreys, summer 1959 (2x2 neg), TARL catalog reference 41ZP92 (5); B, analytical drawings by the author.

# FALCÓN

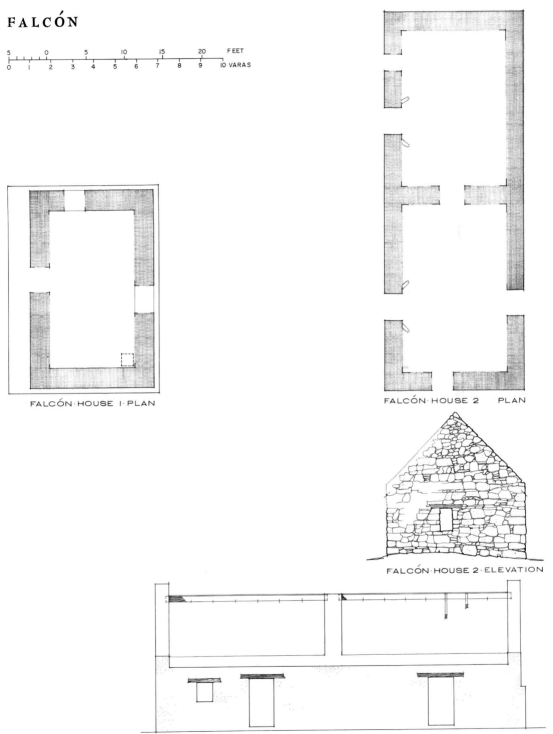

FALCÓN · HOUSE 1 · PLAN

FALCÓN · HOUSE 2    PLAN

FALCÓN · HOUSE 2 · ELEVATION

FALCÓN · HOUSE 2                    ELEVATION WEST

B

**34.** House 1; La Lajita, Zapata County, Texas. A, north elevation; photograph by Bob Humphreys, 1950 (2x2 neg), TARL catalog reference 41ZP88 (15); B, west elevation; photograph by Bob Humphreys(?) 1950 (Fr 2, 4x5 neg), TARL catalog reference 41ZP88 (19); C, southwest corner; photograph by Alex D. Krieger, January 1953 (Fr 33, 35-mm neg), TARL catalog reference 41ZP88 (2); D, north wall fireplace; La Lajita, Zapata County, Texas; photograph by Alex D. Krieger, January 1953 (Fr 1, 35-mm neg), TARL catalog reference 41ZP88(1); E–F, analytical drawings by the author.

C

D

# LA LAJITA

HOUSE 2          PLAN

HOUSE 1          PLAN

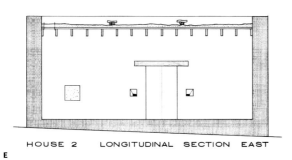

HOUSE 2    LONGITUDINAL SECTION EAST

E

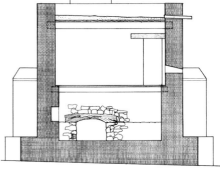

HOUSE 1          LATERAL

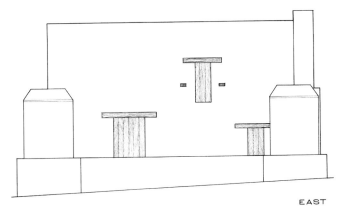

EAST

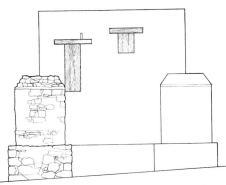

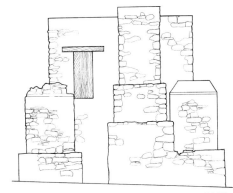

HOUSE I        SOUTH        NORTH        ELEVATIONS

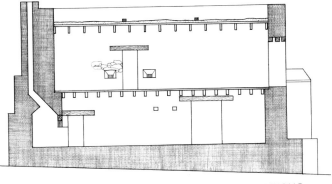

LONGITUDINAL        SECTIONS

F

A

**35.** House 2; Clareño, Zapata County, Texas. A, view southeast; photograph by Alex D. Krieger, January 1953 (Fr 3, 35-mm neg), TARL catalog reference 41ZP89 (1); B, analytical drawings by the author.

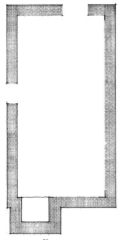

CLAREÑO·HOUSE 2·PLAN

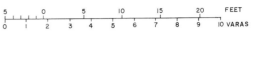

5    0    5    10    15    20    FEET
0  1  2  3  4  5  6  7  8  9  10 VARAS

CLAREÑO·HOUSE 1    PLAN

CLAREÑO · HOUSE 2
ELEVATION   SOUTH

N

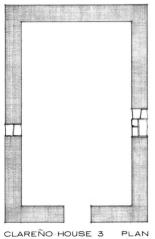

CLAREÑO·HOUSE 3    PLAN

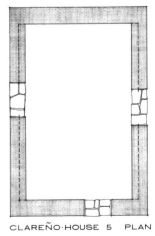

CLAREÑO·HOUSE 5    PLAN

B

**36.** House 4; Clareño, Zapata County, Texas. A, view southwest; photograph by Alex D. Krieger, January 1953 (Fr 6, 35-mm neg), TARL catalog reference 41ZP89(4); B, view northwest; photograph by Alex D. Krieger, January 1953 (35-mm neg), TARL catalog reference 41ZP89; C–D, analytical drawings by the author; E, analytical perspective by Richard Ryan.

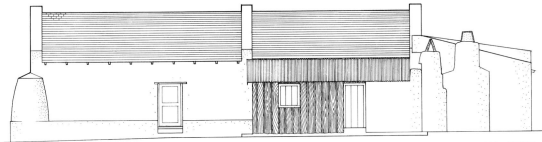

CLAREÑO·HOUSE 4　　　　　　　　　　　　　　　　　　　　　　ELEVATION WEST

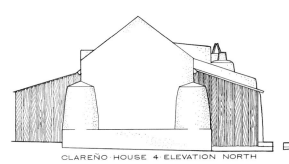

CLAREÑO·HOUSE 4·ELEVATION NORTH

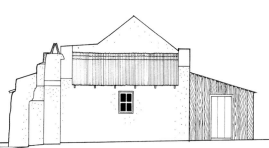

CLAREÑO HOUSE 4·ELEVATION SOUTH

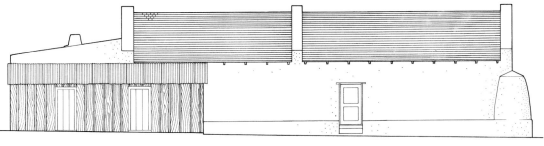

CLAREÑO·HOUSE 4　　　　　　　　　　　　　　　　　　　　　　ELEVATION EAST

C

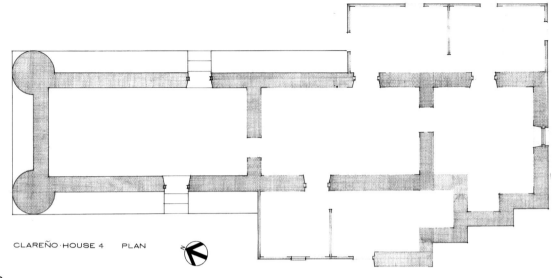

CLAREÑO·HOUSE 4    PLAN

**D**

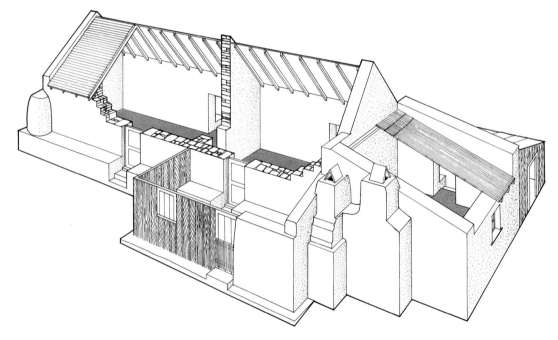

CLAREÑO·HOUSE 4                    ANALYTICAL PERSPECTIVE

**E**

A

**37.** Shrine at the well; El Tigre, Zapata County, Texas. A, photograph attributed to Edward B. Jelks, TARL catalog reference 41ZP91 (C3) (color slide); B, drawing by Katherine Livingston. Scale is approximately one-half inch to the foot.

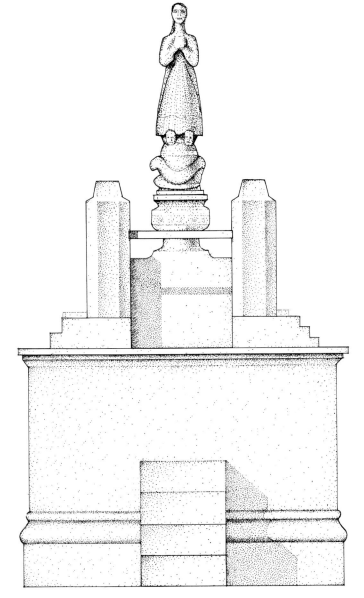

B

One day the floods that had periodically swept the Rio Grande valley and then moved on came to stay. Construction completed, the river was closed at the Falcón Dam on December, 29, 1952, and residents of known low spots began evacuation early in 1953. The reservoir was expected to take three years to fill, so a hasty departure did not seem necessary. A few months later, however, on August 23, surprise rain showers in the watershed caused unanticipated standing water near the villages of Lopeño and Falcón. Feverish evacuation from these sites commenced five days later over slick, muddy roads in a driving rain storm with water rising so rapidly that many treasured possessions were abandoned forever. According to a front page article in the *Laredo Times* of August 29, 1953, probably the last person to leave the area was an elderly man on foot, who with great dignity was "striding along in water up to his chest, on what had formerly been a road toward higher ground, carrying a bundle of clothing and clad simply in underwear shorts." By day's end, a few house-tops, a windmill or two, and the steeple of a church were all that could be seen above the muddy waters.[1]

When the silt-laden waters of the reservoir settled at last, the riparian landscape that had nurtured life through the millennia was no more. Spaces imbued with attachments down through the generations now existed only in memory beneath a flooded region. Whatever opportunities the reservoir might offer, former residents were disoriented both physically and emotionally—bereft of the comfort of familiar landmarks. Whatever the stresses of life during two hundred years of occupancy, the peoples of the Rio Grande had flourished. What these individuals had lost was not just separation from hearth and home but the continuity and harmony of their lives. In the foreword, Ricardo Paz Treviño eloquently related the story of his family. Their experience was repeated a hundred times over by other families.

The flooded towns and ranch sites long buried under the waters of the Falcón Reservoir represent a tragic loss—the loss of significant cultural accomplishments compounded by the trauma of dispossessed persons in their own land. Adherents of the reservoir called Falcón had promised that "scarcity of water in the valley will be a thing of the past. . . . It will be valuable insurance against the floods that have periodically devastated valley lands. . . . It will generate 200,000,000 kilowatt hours of prime electrical energy. . . . The vast lake will provide opportunities for recreation and will be a boon for the economy."[2]

A half a century later those promises are still unfulfilled. The skeptics were right.

**38.** House 4; Clareño, Zapata County, Texas. Photograph by James B. Boyd, 1995–96, 41ZP89.

"Relocation Plan Said Unfair," heralded the *San Antonio Light* on January 24, 1953. "The government is acquiring needlessly 45,000 acres of the most irrigable land and herding people into a new town where they can't make a living." The August 18, 1954, issue of the *Houston Chronicle* proclaimed: "The federal government's failure to deliver on a promise to replace flooded irrigated lands in Zapata County has almost destroyed the economy of the area."

But the worst was yet to come. Construction of the Amistad Reservoir upstream from the Falcón Reservoir, with the potential for controlling the flow of the river downstream began in December 1964, and was completed in November 1969. The lake formed by this action covered 89,000 acres impounding 5.658 million acre feet of water. As at Falcón, Amistad was built for flood control, conservation, irrigation, power, and recreation.[3] Amistad was supposed to release 20,000 cubic feet of water per second, which would stabilize the water level at Falcón. But in the *Zapata County News* dated May 9, 1984, the headline read "Amistad Release Cut Drastically from 20,000 Cubic Feet Promised." The promised release from Amistad was first cut to 13,000, then to 5,000 cubic feet per second.

The Zapatans were in danger of losing their public water supply, and poor water quality created dangerous health problems. Concentrations of raw sewage released from Nuevo Laredo and the pollution from other sources in Mexico compounded

**39.** House 3, canned goods cache; Clareño Ranch, Zapata County, Texas.
Photograph by James B. Boyd, 1995–96, 41ZP89.

**40.** Old wagon emerging from the lake at Santaneno Ranch, Zapata County, Texas. Photograph by James B. Boyd, August 1996, 1995–96, 41ZP298.

the crisis. In one test sample of the water, the presence of heavy noncoliform bacteria was identified. That the water was declared "unsuitable" but safe was hardly reassuring. Two consecutive years of kill of fish spawn seriously reduced the tourist industry. As the lake level receded, the bare shorelines revealed a desert devoid of life.

The crisis generated by the Amistad was exacerbated by droughts of historic proportions in the Rio Grande Basin: the three-year drought that began in 1983—the period of my initial visits to the towns long flooded by the Falcón Reservoir—and the drought of the mid-1990s that finally ended in 2004.[4]

As the lake levels receded the first time, ghostly remains of the town of old Zapata reemerged, offering the opportunity to commemorate all that was lost. "Domingo en la Plaza to Be Held in Ruins of Old Zapata" announced the *Zapata County News* on May 12, 1983. The event took place thirty years after the closing of the dam to form the Falcón Reservoir. It happened on a Sunday evening on the tennis court in the vicinity of the plaza. Celebrants were warned not to drive off the discernable roadways since dangerous open cisterns still lurked beneath the surface. The physical past that had been severed from living experience was again palpable. It was a homecoming. Parents could show children remnants of the family home, places where one had entered and sat by the fire on a cold night, places known to their grandparents, places where they had been born, places where they had known the joys and sorrows of life. They had once been part of a place that for thirty years had no existence. Many wept.

But with the exposure of the historic sites each time the waters of the reservoir receded even farther came the looters and scavengers: "The frenzied activities of the looters and collectors have damaged and/or destroyed an untold number of archaeological sites at Falcón Reservoir threatening the very fabric of the prehistoric and historic cultural heritage of this part of the Rio Grande Valley and calling into question whether the material expression of this heritage can be preserved and protected for future generations to appreciate and study."[5] These sites are again "safely buried" but for how long?

Wallace Gillpatrick wrote in *The Man Who Likes Mexico* that, although more than four hundred years had passed, "in the dwellings of the Spanish Moors in Africa there still hang massive keys to their lost homes in Granada and that for generations they cherished the hope to return."[6] Such is man's love of home.

Of all the towns and settlements along the Rio Grande founded by José de Escandón in the mid-eighteenth century, Revilla, renamed Guerrero then later Guerrero Viejo, was far and away the grandest.[1] The forty families from Coahuila that formed the nucleus of the colonial town burgeoned to a population of forty thousand by the mid-nineteenth century. The Hotel Flores was long a center of elegant social activity. Until 1871 a continuous balcony circled around the second story—the ballroom where dancing and celebrations were held to the accompaniment of the Flores family orchestra. On the ground floor, a shop sold imported European goods shipped up the Rio Grande by steamboat from New Orleans. Alas, by the time the floods came in 1953, only twenty-five hundred residents remained. Wars and political unrest contributed to the population decline as did the construction of the federal railroad from Monterrey to Laredo.

After partial inundation by the Falcón Reservoir, the town was abandoned—battered by wave action, harsh climatic conditions, and looters and vandals who carted away the stones. In recent decades, as the reservoir level fluctuated periodically, the remains of the old town became an attraction for tourists and other less benign company. Although the Mexican government has attempted to protect the historic site—stabilizing the church—they have been no more successful in enforcing the laws against looting than have U.S. law enforcement officials. Maria Eugenia Guerra, eminent borderlands journalist, observed in 2006: "All the attention drawn to the old town-site and its accessibility along a well-maintained road has given the place another look, another feel, and yet that powerful, engaging beauty radiates, persists. . . . That beauty, so evident in the precise cuts of stones speaks far more powerfully than words to say that no acts of men—then in so massive a measure as condemnation and inundation or now in plundering and disregard—can alter the soul of this place called Guerrero Viejo."[2]

### HISTORY REVEALED, HISTORY DESTROYED

The severe drought of the mid-1990s dramatically dropped the water level of the Falcón Reservoir to reveal historic towns, ranch sites, churches, and cemeteries—some dating from the eighteenth century—as well as Indian artifacts and burial sites that archaeologists say may date back eleven thousand years. The reservoir had then reached record lows, fifty feet below normal. Covering eighty-seven thousand acres when filled, it shrank to some twenty thousand acres. Posted signs warned

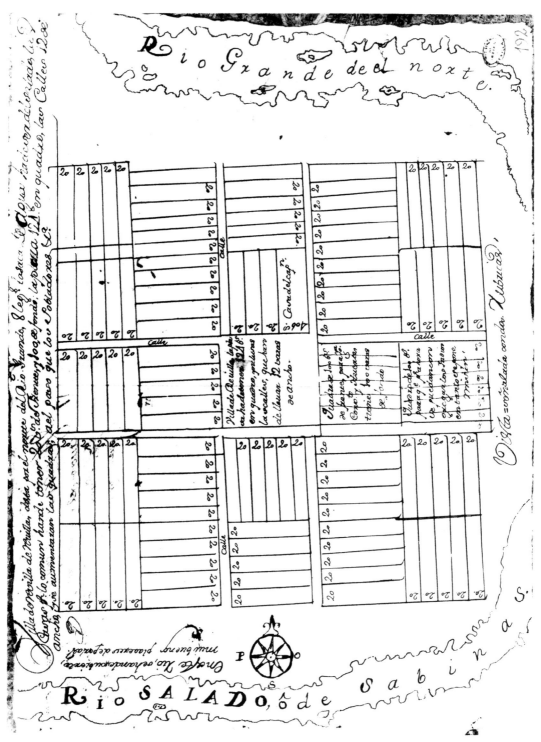

**41.** A 1751 map from Archivo General de Indias, Seville, Spain: Mexico Item 192 (1751) Plano de la Villa de Revilla, 1751. Courtesy Spanish Ministry of Culture.

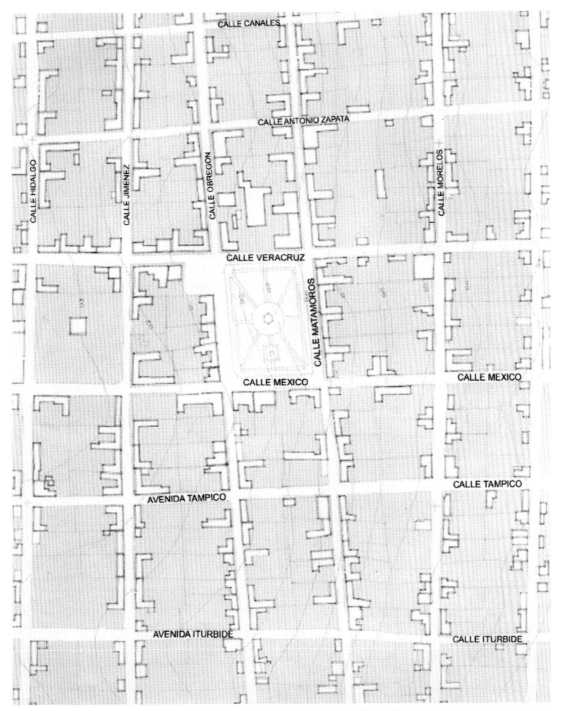

**42.** Town plat, Revilla (Guerrero Viejo). Section bounded (*clockwise*) by Calle Canales, Calle Morelos, Avenida Iturbe, and Calle Hidalgo. Redrawn from a 1943 tax map by staff in the author's office.

**43.** Street scene; Revilla (Guerrero Viejo). The Hotel Flores (*right*) abuts the plaza. There have been additional wall collapses since 1994. Photograph by the author, September 30, 1994, from the approximate position of the photograph made forty-five years earlier (Fig. 11).

**44.** House in Revilla (Guerrero Viejo). Photograph by the author, September 30, 1994.

**45.** The masons of Guerrero Viejo were famed throughout the region for their skill in the construction of arches. Photograph by the author, August 18, 1983.

against removal of artifacts but looters continued to pilfer and damage relics uncovered by the receding reservoir.

> NOTICE: Ancient ruins, archaeological resources, fossils, and historical remnants in the vicinity of this notice are fragile and irreplaceable. The Antiquities Act of 1906 and the Archaeological Resources Protection Act of 1979 protect them for the benefit of all Americans. ENJOY BUT DO NOT DESTROY YOUR AMERICAN HERITAGE. DO NOT DIG, REMOVE, INJURE, OR DESTROY ANY HISTORIC OR PREHISTORIC OBJECTS, RUINS, OR SITES. Violators subject to arrest, a maximum fine of $20,000, and/or imprisonment. United States Department of Antiquities–Forest Service.

The American Antiquities Act sought to suppress vandalism, commercialized plundering, and the destruction of southwestern Indian sites that had been going on since the 1890s. Since the Falcón sites are part of the public domain; the act is applicable.[3]

In mid-August 1996, a major research project was instituted. A team of archaeologists and mapping specialists from the Texas Archaeological Research Laboratory, the Texas Historical Commission, the National Park Service, the Southern Texas Archaeological Association, and the Texas Archaeological Stewards Network seized

**46.** Small, closely spaced rectangular blocks known as dentils—used especially in classical architecture—were carved into the cornice stones of a building on Matamoras Street in Guerrero Viejo. Photograph by the author, August 18, 1983.

**47.** Ornamental relief later stolen by looters. Photograph by the author, August 18, 1983.

**48.** Ornamental relief later stolen by looters. Photograph by the author August 18, 1983.

**49.** Classical Corinthian capital later stolen by looters. When it was photographed by the author, August 18, 1983, it retained remnants of polychromy.

the opportunity for a week's study in the field.[4] That looters, plunderers, and vandals were at work was everywhere evident. The program designed by the research team included identifying sites, satellite mapping of positions of various features associated with the sites, studying design and construction of buildings, photographing features revealed in the process, marking positions of features for further study and analysis, and minimal collecting of artifacts for study. Of course, the required permits were obtained to enter the sites from the private owner or the responsible agency—in this case, the International Boundary and Water Commission, a Mexican and U.S. agency that manages the Rio Grande. If artifacts were collected for study and display, permission was stated in the permit. If these were on privately owned property, the owner retained ownership and was advised concerning their proper documentation and preservation. State officials have criticized the underfunded IBWC for neglecting its responsibility to preserve the area's historic sites.[5]

Early phases of the 1996 Falcón study included an overview of the area, prior to flagging specific sites or features for intensive recording and analysis. Tragically, marking the sites for study also identified valuables for the looters. Late one night in the course of the investigation while the research team was absent, one cemetery was feverishly excavated by looters. Piles of earth were strewn about the site in an attempt to get to the burials beneath. Crowning one mound of earth was a child's

**50.** Nuestra Señora del Refugio, facing the plaza; Revilla (Guerrero Viejo), built after 1801. Photograph by the author, September 30, 1994.

**51.** When the water was high in Lake Falcón, fishermen in boats were able to inscribe their names above the springing of the arches in the church interior. During periods of drought, goats belonging to Julia Zamora—often the lone occupant of the town—found refuge there in the heat of the day. Photograph by the author, August 1983.

**52.** The author in the plaza where orchestras in the bandstand once serenaded young men and women during their evening promenade. Photograph by Mary Carolyn George, August 18, 1983.

wooden casket. The casket, ornamented by painted geometric designs, appeared to have been made from cypress, a durable hardwood, which accounted for its survival. The casket from the Falcón area, though larger, was similar to one depicted in a painting by Theodore Gentilz, *Entierro de un Ángel* (in the permanent collection of the Daughters of the Republic of Texas Library at the Alamo.) On viewing the casket, one felt the grief of a family so long ago. That the burial, assumed to be timeless, would be so desecrated was unthinkable. Yet it is rumored that human bones were and are marketable, especially the skull of a child.

The multidisciplinary research project of 1996 resulted in a substantial quantity of cultural knowledge. What seemed evident was that the occupants of the Falcón vicinity had for two centuries responded responsibly to the challenges of the land, maintained continuity through generations of occupancy, and given character to a culture: an example worthy of emulation.[6]

**SALVAGE FIELD STUDIES AND THE PARTICIPANTS INVOLVED, 1949–1952**

During the winter of 1948–49, the Smithsonian Institution, through its River Basin Surveys (Frank H. H. Roberts Jr., chief), and the Santa Fe office of the National Park Service (Erik K. Reed, archaeologist) were informed of the site location for the new Falcón Reservoir. The destruction of cultural artifacts within the reservoir area caused by the impounding of water, the displacement of the affected population, and the major changes in the lives of those displaced were concerns shared by these agencies.[1]

In early February 1949, anthropologist Alex D. Krieger of the University of Texas at Austin made an inspection trip to the vicinity of the proposed dam. He identified six significant sites, all to be destroyed in the initial construction phase.[2] The U.S. Department of State and the National Park Service funded the critical salvage field studies. Krieger returned to the area for another survey in July 1949, this time with a Harvard geologist, Kirk Bryan, and Jack T. Hughes, a student in the Anthropology Department, University of Texas. Glen L. Evans, a geologist with the Texas Memorial Museum, also visited the area and reported that clearing then under way was damaging several sensitive sites. In March 1950, the University of Texas made contractual arrangements for archaeological field surveys with the National Park Service. Under the direction of Alex Krieger, a crew headed by Bob Humphreys was placed in the field through the summer months of 1950. Liaison was established between Krieger and Luis Areleyra Arroyo de Anda of the National Institute of Anthropology and History, Mexico, D.F., and field observations were jointly made during July 1950.[3] At the same time, Benjamin C. Tharp, a professor of botany, and William Blair, a zoologist who undertook mammalian studies—both at the University of Texas—conducted research in the area. Additional studies by Robert S. Ravicz concerned the history and ethnology of the Coahuiltecan Indians. Herbert Klose evaluated artifacts from the historic sites.[4]

In the investigations of the valley floor of what was to become the Falcón Reservoir, the prehistoric Native Americans who occupied the area for thousands of years prior to the arrival of Spanish colonists were the primary interest. There was confusion concerning site inquiry because Spanish cultural materials that often overlaid prehistoric materials were frequently overlooked in order to retrieve prehistoric data. More than a decade would pass following initial work at Falcón before scientific inquiry at historic sites became the norm.[5]

Susceptible to immediate damage early in 1951 due to proximity to the dam construction, three sites near Ramireño (also known as El Ramireño del Abajo) became the focus of emergency crews placed in the field under the direction of Donald D. Hartle.[6] Following in the wake of previous digs, the 1952 season of salvage operations began in mid-January and lasted until the end of May.[7] Joe F. Cason of the University of Texas maintained three notebooks during this phase of the work. Notebook one contained archaeological notes describing various sites within the boundaries of the future reservoir. Notebook two was Cason's field diary. Rough line sketches of historic buildings and genealogical data pertinent to ranching families associated with the settlements were included in the third notebook. Alex Krieger, Jack T. Hughes, Bob Humphreys, and others who have not been identified, photographed the buildings. The work was put in perspective by a passage from Joe Cason's notebooks: "A study of an area through time . . . which would show man's relation to his environment . . . including . . . successive life patterns of the aboriginal population, the colonial Spanish, and the present inhabitants . . . would result in considerable knowledge concerning a relatively unknown area. In addition, the continuity of the historical approach would render the status of the area's present population understandable in terms of its past and have considerable bearing upon the efficacy of alternative choices or reorientation after displacement."[8] With this challenge, but without funding, in 1961 I began additional archival and field research that yielded a series of drawings of dwellings identified in Joe Cason's third notebook. In order to complete and publish the architectural information gained from this lengthy process, I requested a grant in October 1975. The Texas Historical Foundation in conjunction with the Texas Historical Commission responded generously, which resulted in the publication of *Historic Architecture of Texas: The Falcón Reservoir*.

**INTRODUCTION**

1. This statement introduced a slide-tape presentation I made titled "Architecture of the Rio Grande," which was sponsored by the Texas Historical Commission and distributed in English and Spanish versions to the schoolchildren of Texas in 1979. The Texas Historical Commission subsequently initiated the Los Caminos del Rio Heritage Project in 1990, conceived by architect Mario L. Sánchez. Today, a two-hundred-mile region functions as one continuous international heritage corridor. In commemoration of the Christopher Columbus Quincentenary, the Historical Commission has also published several guides to encourage cultural tourism; they are listed in the references.

2. Leon C. Metz, s.v.v. "Rio Grande," in *New Handbook of Texas.*

3. Florence Johnson Scott, *Historical Heritage of the Lower Rio Grande* (Waco, Texas: Texian Press, 1966), 67–68.

4. For a discussion of materials usage in a broader geographic area, see Joe C. Freeman, "Regional Architecture and Associated Crafts," in *A Shared Experience,* ed. Mario L. Sánchez (Austin: Los Caminos del Rio Heritage Project and the Texas Historical Commission, 1994), 184–86.

5. For a discussion of the use of caliche block, see Mary Anna Casstevens, "Randado: The Built Environment of a Texas-Mexican Ranch," in *Hecho en Tejas,* ed. Joe S. Graham (Denton: University of North Texas Press, 1991), 309–17.

6. Vernacular architecture achieved respect—long withheld but richly deserved—with the exhibition Architecture without Architects at the Museum of Modern Art in New York City, November 1964–February 1965, and the accompanying publication of the same name by the guest curator Bernard Rudofsky. In the course of replicating a nineteenth-century adobe structure as part of the folklife exhibit area at the Institute of Texan Cultures in San Antonio, I gained a deeper appreciation of vernacular borderlands buildings and their builders. Carmen Orozco, the contractor and his crew who came from Presidio in the Trans-Pecos region of southwest Texas, were indispensable to the successful outcome of the project, as was master mason Curtis Hunt who prepared the stone foundation. Although located immediately adjacent to Interstate 37 and across from the Alamodome, the thirty-inch thick walls provide a cool, quiet haven, even in midsummer.

7. Patsy Jeanne Byfield, *Falcón Dam and the Lost Towns of Zapata* (Austin: Texas Memorial Museum, 1971). Dick D. Heller Jr., s.v.v. "International Falcón Reservoir," in *New Handbook of Texas.* Of the three dams originally authorized by the U.S.-Mexico Water Treaty of 1944, two have been completed: the International Falcón Reservoir (1954) and the Amistad Dam and Reservoir near Del Rio (1969). Though beyond the scope of this

book, the machinations that attended the Falcón Reservoir, indeed all "big water" projects, are well documented.

8. William Clayton Barbee, "A Historical and Architectural Investigation of San Ignacio, Texas" (master's thesis, University of Texas at Austin, 1981). Research for Barbee's thesis was conducted over two years, with extended periods of residency in San Ygnacio. The documentation of extant buildings ca. 1980 established a baseline for subsequent studies of the town. See, for example, Dick D. Heller Jr., s.v.v. "San Ygnacio, Texas," in *New Handbook of Texas; A Shared Experience,* ed. Sanchez; and Helen Simons and Cathryn A. Hoyt, eds., *A Guide to Hispanic Texas* (Austin: University of Texas Press, 1984), 113–17. San Ygnacio Historic District, San Ygnacio, Zapata County, Texas: Documentation for listing on the National Register of Historic Places, U.S. Department of the Interior and the National Park Service. On file at Texas Historical Commission Library.

9. The first national acknowledgment of the treasure that is San Ygnacio likely appeared in I. T. Frary, "Picturesque Towns of the Border Land," *Architectural Record* (Apr. 1919): 382–84.

10. Statement of significance transmitted to me by Judy George-Garza, History Programs Division, Texas Historical Commission.

11. In *Historical Heritage of the Lower Rio Grande Valley* (123–75), Florence Johnson Scott documents both legal and historical issues confronting early pioneers in the borderlands.

12. Martha Doty Freeman, *Fort Sam Houston: An American Depot, Headquarters, and Training Facility, 1876–1946* (Fort Worth: Komatsu/Rangel, 1994), 15–45.

13. When I first visited the Treviño-Uribe fortified house in 1961 in the company of Florence Johnson Scott, it was the residence of María Herrera, a descendant of the Uribe family, who extended hospitality and provided information that contributed to a better understanding of the settlements recently submerged beneath the Falcón Reservoir.

14. Eugene George, "Medina River Ranch," *Fine Homebuilding* (Spring 1987): 66–71.

**CHAPTER 1. THE SETTLEMENTS IN NUEVO SANTANDER**

1. David M. Vigness, "The Lower Rio Grande Valley. 1836–1846" (master's thesis, University of Texas, Austin, 1948), 3–4.

2. Lawrence Francis Hill, *José de Escandón and the Founding of Nuevo Santander* (Columbus: Ohio State University Press, 1926), 34.

3. Alex D. Krieger and Jack T. Hughes, Archaeological Salvage in the Falcón Reservoir Area, Progress Report No. 1, report to the National Park Service, 1950, on file at TARL, Balcones Research Center, University of Texas at Austin, 14.

4. Closner Ramsey, "Scrapbook of the Lower Rio Grande Valley," in my possession, 57.

5. Vigness, "Lower Rio Grande Valley," 4–5; Hill, *José de Escandón,* 5; and *Our Catholic Heritage in Texas, 1519–1936,* prepared under the Auspices of the Knights of Columbus of Texas, by Carlos E. Castañeda (Austin: Von Boeckmann-Jones, 1936), 3:137–39.

6. Robert Weddle, s.v.v. "Nuevo Santander," in *New Handbook of Texas.*

7. Hill, *José de Escandón,* 51–66.

8. Vigness, "Lower Rio Grande Valley," 7

9. Frank C. Pierce, *A Brief History of the Lower Rio Grande Valley* (Menasha, Wisc.: George Banta Publishing, 1917), 22.

10. Hill, *José de Escandón,* 89–100.

11. José Roberto Juarez Jr., "An Architectural Description of Dolores Ranch," typescript, 1976. Also by the same author, "Day at Dolores," typescript, 1977. The Dolores Ranch was founded in 1859 by Cosme Martinez, the great-great-great grandfather of Juarez. The land for the ranch was purchased from the heirs of the José Borrego land grant. The family built the last house on the ranch in 1914. The two reports are in my possession.

### CHAPTER 2. THE LAND AND ITS UTILIZATION

1. Curry Holden, "Fray Vicente Santa Maria: Historical Account of the Colony of Nuevo Santander and the Coast of the Seno Mexicano" (master's thesis, University of Texas, Austin, 1924), 25–40.

2. Maximilian, Baron von Alvensleben, *With Maximilian in Mexico* (London: Longmans, Green, 1867), 60.

3. Quotation from the *Dallas Morning News,* date and page number lost.

4. Emmanuel Domenech, *Missionary Adventures in Texas and Mexico* (London: Longman, Brown, Green, Longmans, and Roberts, 1858), 269–70.

5. Lewis Mumford, *Sticks and Stones: A Study of American Architecture and Civilization* (New York: Harcourt, Brace, and World, 1955), preface to 2nd ed., n.p.

6. Hill, *José de Escandón,* 132.

7. Dan Stanislawski, "Early Spanish Town Planning," *Geographical Review* 38 (1947): 96.

8. Hill, *José de Escandón,* 130–32.

9. Pierce, *Brief History,* 22–25.

10. Holden, "Fray Vicente," 38.

11. Herbert Eugene Bolton, "Tienda de Cuervo's Ynspección of Laredo, 1757," *Texas State Historical Association Quarterly* 6, no. 2 (June 1903): 187–203.

12. Hill, *José de Escandón,* 133.

13. J. Frank Dobie, *The Longhorns* (Boston: Little, Brown, 1941), 21.

14. Pierce, *Brief History,* 22–25.

15. J. Frank Dobie, *Coronado's Children* (Garden City, N.Y.: Garden City Publishing, 1930), 21.

### CHAPTER 3. BUILDING TECHNOLOGY

1. A. T. Myrthe [pseud.], *Ambrosio de Letinez; or, the First Texian Novel,* facsimile of 1842 ed. (Austin: Steck, 1967), 1:84.

2. For a more extensive discussion of the jacal, see Joe S. Graham, "The Jacal in South Texas," in *Hecho en Tejas,* ed. Joe S. Graham (Denton: University of North Texas Press, 1991), 293–99.

3. Alex D. Krieger, an archaeologist who documented buildings soon to be buried beneath the waters of the Falcón Reservoir, also photographed prototypical buildings in Vallecillo, Nuevo Leon, Mexico, which lies midway between Laredo, Texas, and Monterrey, Mexico (illustrations 14–15 and 22–24). A town of mining origin, Real de San Carlos de Vallecillo was founded in 1768 and colonized by Spaniards interested in finding silver. Built of locally quarried dark gray limestone, the town has long been admired by architecture aficionados who were concerned that this historic treasure, though virtually intact, was in decline due to decades of abandonment and neglect. Beginning in the 1980s, a conservation and preservation program under the direction of architect Javier Sánchez Garcia for the Department of Anthropology and History of Nuevo Leon has given new life to the town. Stabilization of the church, enhancement of the plaza, and other measures have engendered a sense of community pride and a raised awareness of the importance of Vallecillo. Stone from the ancient quarry was still available in 2006, according to architect E. Logan Wagner.

4. Virgil N. Lott and Mercurio Martinez, *The Kingdom of Zapata* (San Antonio: Naylor, 1953), 129–35.

5. E. Boyd, *Popular Arts of Spanish New Mexico* (Santa Fe: Museum of Santa Fe Press, 1974), 23.

6. Mrs. V. K. Carpenter, *State of Texas Federal Population Schedules, Seventh Census of the United States, 1850* (Huntsville, Ark.: Century Enterprises, 1969), 326.

7. Ramsey, "Scrapbook," 57, 76.

8. Krieger and Hughes, *Archaeological Salvage*, 12.

9. Holden, "Fray Vicente," 74. Unlike its tropical relatives, the Texas ebony, or ébano, mentioned by Fray Vicente has a dark red, not black, heartwood. Robert A. Vines, *Trees, Shrubs, and Woody Vines of the Southwest* (Austin: University of Texas Press, 1960) is an invaluable reference for this type of information.

10. Krieger and Hughes, *Archaeological Salvage*, 12.

11. Hill, *José de Escandón*, 130.

## CHAPTER 4. DESCRIPTIONS OF LIFE IN THE BORDERLANDS

1. Myrthe [pseud.], *Ambrosio de Letinez*, 96–97.

2. W. H. Emory, *Notes of a Military Reconnaissance from Fort Leavenworth, in Missouri, to San Diego, in California, Including Parts of the Arkansas, Del Norte, and Gila Rivers* (Washington, D.C.: 1848), 39–40.

3. Frederick Law Olmsted, *A Journey through Texas* (New York: Dix, Edwards, 1857), 346–49.

4. David Montejano, *Anglos and Mexicans in the Making of Texas, 1836–1986* (Austin: University of Texas Press, 1987). Andrés Tijerina, *Tejanos and Texas under the Mexican Flag, 1831–1836* (College Station: Texas A&M University Press, 1994).

5. Montejano, *Anglos and Mexicans*, 104.

6. Jovita González, "Social Life in Cameron, Starr, and Zapata Counties" (master's thesis,

University of Texas at Austin, 1930), 69. González's *Dew on the Thorn,* edited by José Limón (Houston, Texas: Arte Público Press, 1997), was based on material from her thesis.

7. Emilia Schunior Ramírez, *Ranch Life in Hidalgo County after 1850* (Edinburg, Texas: New Santander Press, 1971), part 6, n.p.

8. González, "Social Life," 66–67.

9. Eugene George, "Pierre Yves Keralum, O.M.I.: Architect for God on the Texas Border," *Journal of Texas Catholic History and Culture* 6 (1995): 35–46.

10. Paul Horgan, *The Devil in the Desert* (New York: Longmans, Green, 1952).

11. Robert E. Wright, O.M.I., s.v.v. "Pierre Yves Keralum," in *New Handbook of Texas.*


### CHAPTER 6. HOMELAND LOST

1. Quotation is from the *Laredo Times.* For a general discussion of the evacuation, see Byfield, Falcón Dam.

2. Don Hinga, "Dam Will End Valley Water Scarcity," *Houston Chronicle,* Dec. 16, 1952, B1.

3. Christopher Long, s.v.v. "Amistad Reservoir," in *New Handbook of Texas.*

4. "Falcón Lake Benefits from Flooding in Mexico, Rains in South Texas," May 10, 2004, Texas Parks and Wildlife Web site, www.tpwd.state.tx.us/newsmedia/releases/?req=20040510b.

5. Tim Pertula, quoted in "The Falcon Sites: Present and Past Destruction," Texas beyond History, www.texasbeyondhistory.net/falcon/destruction.html.

6. Wallace Gillpatrick, *The Man Who Likes Mexico* (New York: Century, 1912), 91–92.


### EPILOGUE: GUERRERO VIEJO

1. Much has been written about Revilla/Guerrero Viejo in recent decades. Among the sources used in the epilogue are John Ward Anderson, "Old City Emerges from Reservoir," *Washington Post,* May 24, 1998, A25–30; Rubén Flores Gutierrez, "Guerrero Viejo: An Architectural Legacy" in *A Shared Experience,* ed. Mario L. Sánchez, 2nd ed. (Austin: Los Caminos del Rio Heritage Project and the Texas Historical Commission, 1994), 199–223 (also online at www.rice.edu/armadillo/Past/); Lori Brown McVey, *Guerrero Viejo: A Photographic Essay* (Laredo, Tex.: Nuevo Santander Museum Complex, 1988).

2. From a telephone conversation between Maria Eugenia Guerra and Mary Carolyn George.

3. A history of the Antiquities Act as well as links to other sites about the act can be found at www.cr.nps.gov/history/hisnps/npshistory/antiq.htm. The full act can be read at www.cr.nps.gov/local-law/anti1906.htm. Concerns for ethical practice reach international levels. A UNESCO convention includes directions "to implement the Convention on the Means of Prohibiting and Preventing the Illicit Import, Export and Transfer of Cultural Property."

4. Pertula, "The Falcon Sites."

5. James E. Garcia, "History Revealed," *Austin American Statesman,* Aug. 20, 1996, A1.

6. Pertula, "The Falcon Sites."


**APPENDIX: CULTURAL INQUIRY**

1. Krieger and Hughes, *Archaeological Salvage,* 3; Joe F. Cason, "Falcón Reservoir Notebooks," 3 vols., MSS, 1952, on file at TARL, University of Texas at Austin, 7.

2. Krieger and Hughes, *Archaeological Salvage,* 3.

3. Luis Aveleyra Arroyo de Anda, "Reconocimiento Arquelógico en la Zona de La Presa Internacional Falcón, Tamaulipas y Texas," *Revista Mexicana de Estudios Antropológicos* 7 (1951): 31–59.

4. Krieger and Hughes, *Archaeological Salvage,* 6.

5. Edward Jelks, "The Founding Meeting of the Society for Historical Archaeology, 6 January 1967," *Journal of the Society for Historical Archaeology* 27, no. 1 (1993), 10–11.

6. Donald D. Hartle and Robert L. Stephenson, *Archaeological Excavations at the Falcón Reservoir, Starr County, Texas,* River Basin Surveys (Washington, D.C.: Smithsonian Institution, 1951), on file at TARL, University of Texas at Austin.

7. Cason, "Falcón Reservoir Notebooks," Jan. 19–May 31, 1952.

8. Cason, "Falcón Reservoir Notebooks," Jan. 19–May 31, 1952. Concerning Joe Cason, the archaeologist Alex Krieger said, "I just remember that Joe could not operate a camera, but he was very good on a bagpipe, much to the astonishment of the Mexicans on both sides of the river."

# References

In the course of my work on *Historic Architecture of Texas: The Falcón Reservoir,* I found that the available resources were relatively few and often obscure. The help of university librarians and archivists was often needed to gain access. Those references are indicated by an asterisk at the end of an entry. In recent decades, interest in all aspects of borderlands culture has burgeoned, generating numerous publications. In addition, sources may be accessed through modern information technology. Such materials have been used to supplement the references used in *Historic Architecture.* Research materials and drawings used in preparation of *Lost Architecture of the Rio Grande Borderlands* have been deposited with the W. Eugene George Papers, Nettie Lee Benson Latin American Collection, University of Texas Libraries, University of Texas at Austin.

Alvensleben, Maximilian, Baron von. *With Maximilian in Mexico.* London: Longmans, Green, 1867.*

Anderson, John Ward. "Old City Emerges from Reservoir." *Washington Post,* May 24, 1998, A25–30.

Aveleyra Arroya de Anda, Luis. "Reconocimiento Arquelógico en la Zona de la Presa Internacional Falcón, Tamaulipas y Texas." *Revista Mexicana de Estudios Antropológicos* 7 (1951): 31–59.*

Barbee, William Clayton. "A Historical and Architectural Investigation of San Ignacio, Texas." Master's thesis, University of Texas at Austin, 1981.

Barbee, William Clayton, and Jorge Pardo. "The Proceso Martínez House, San Ignacio, Texas." Report, University of Texas at Austin, 1979.

Bolton, Herbert Eugene. *Texas in the Middle Eighteenth Century: Studies in Spanish Colonial History and Administration.* New York: Russell and Russell, 1962.*

———. "Tienda de Cuervo's *Ynspección* of Laredo, 1757." *Texas State Historical Association Quarterly* 6, no. 2 (June 1903): 187–201.*

Boyd, E. *Popular Arts of Spanish New Mexico.* Santa Fe.: Museum of Santa Fe Press, 1974.*

Byfield, Patsy Jeanne. *The Falcón Dam and the Lost Towns of Zapata.* Austin: Texas Memorial Museum, 1971.*

Carpenter, Mrs. V. K., transcriber. *The State of Texas Federal Population Schedules, Seventh Census of the United States, 1850.* 5 vols. Huntsville, Ark.: Century Enterprises, 1969.*

Cason, Joe F. "Falcón Reservoir Notebooks." 3 vols. MSS, 1952. On file at the Texas Archaeological Research Laboratory (TARL), University of Texas at Austin.*

———. "Report on Archaeological Salvage in Falcón Reservoir, Season of 1952." *Bulletin of the Texas Archaeological and Paleontological Society* 23 (1953): 218–59.*

Casstevens, Mary Anna. "Randado: The Built Environment of a Texas-Mexican Ranch."

In *Hecho en Tejas,* ed. Joe S. Graham, 309–17. Denton: University of North Texas Press, 1991.

Curliss, J. Andrew. "Drying Reservoir Reveals History." *Boston Sunday Globe,* Sept. 15, 1996, A-23.

———. "Uncovering History: Shrinking Valley Reservoir Draws Researchers, Looters." *Dallas Morning News,* Aug. 23, 1996, 1–33A.

DeLong, David G. Introduction to *Historic American Buildings: Texas.* Vols. 1–2. New York: Garland Publishing, 1979.

Dobie, J. Frank. *Coronado's Children.* Garden City, N.Y.: Garden City Publishing, 1930.*

———. *The Longhorns.* Boston: Little, Brown, 1941.*

Domenech, Emmanuel. *Missionary Adventures in Texas and Mexico.* London: Longman, Brown, Green, Longmans, and Roberts, 1858.*

Emory, W. H. *Notes of a Military Reconnaissance, from Fort Leavenworth, in Missouri, to San Diego, in California, Including Parts of the Arkansas, Del Norte, and Gila Rivers.* Washington, D.C., 1848.*

Fish, Jean Y. *Zapata County Roots Revisited.* Edinburg, Tex.: New Santander Press, 1990.

Fish, Robert W., compiler. *A Preliminary Index of Spanish-Mexican Land Grants in Zapata County, Texas.* Zapata, Tex.: Zapata County Historical Society, 1986.

Flores Gutierrez, Rubén. "Guerrero Viejo: An Architectural Legacy." In *A Shared Experience,* ed. Mario L. Sánchez. 2nd ed. Austin: Los Caminos del Rio Heritage Project and the Texas Historical Commission, 1994. Information may also be accessed online at http://www.rice.edu/armadillo/Past/.

Frary, I. T. "Picturesque Towns of the Border Land." *Architectural Record* (Apr. 1919): 382–84.

Freeman, Martha Doty. *Fort Sam Houston: An American Depot, Headquarters, and Training Facility, 1876–1946.* Fort Worth: Komatsu/Rangel, 1994.

Garcia, James E. "History Revealed: Looters Rush in as Drought Exposes Artifacts along Falcón Reservoir." *Austin American-Statesman,* Aug. 20, 1996, A1.

George, W. Eugene. *Historic Architecture of Texas: The Falcón Reservoir.* Austin: Texas Historical Commission and Texas Historical Foundation, 1975.

———. "Medina River Ranch." *Fine Homebuilding* (Spring 1987): 66–71.

———. "Pierre Yves Keralum, O.M.I.: Architect for God on the Texas Border." *Journal of Texas Catholic History and Culture* 6 (1995): 35–46.

Gillpatrick, Wallace. *The Man Who Likes Mexico.* New York: Century, 1912.

González, Jovita. *Dew on the Thorn.* Ed. José Limón. Houston: Arte Público Press, 1997.

———. "Social Life in Cameron, Starr, and Zapata Counties." Master's thesis, University of Texas at Austin, 1930.

Graham, Joe S. *El Rancho in South Texas.* Denton: University of North Texas Press for John E. Conner Museum, Texas A&M University, 1994.

———. "The Jacal in South Texas." In *Hecho en Tejas,* ed. Joe S. Graham, 293–99. Denton: University of North Texas Press, 1991.

Guerra, María Eugenia. "Nothing to Declare." In *Rio Grande,* ed Jan Reid, 231–41. Austin: University of Texas Press, 2004.

———. "Will the IBWC Rise to the Task of Protecting Antiquities of the Falcón Reservoir?" *LareDOS* (Sept. 1996): 6–7.

Hartle, Donald D., and Robert L. Stephenson. *Archaeological Excavations at the Falcón Reservoir, Starr County, Texas.* River Basin Surveys. Washington, D.C.: Smithsonian Institution, 1951. On file at the Texas Archaeological Research Laboratory (TARL), University of Texas at Austin*

Hill, Lawrence Francis. *José de Escandón and the Founding of Nuevo Santander.* Columbus: Ohio State University Press, 1926.*

Hinga, Don. "Dam Will End Valley Water Scarcity." *Houston Chronicle,* Dec. 16, 1952, B1.

Holden, William Curry. "Fray Vicente Santa Maria: Historical Account of the Colony of Nuevo Santander and the Coast of the Seno Mexicano with Introduction and Annotations." Master's thesis, University of Texas, Austin, 1924.*

Horgan, Paul. *The Devil in the Desert.* New York: Longmans, Green, 1952.

Houghton, Adele. "Internal Frontier: Spanish Colonial Architecture along the Rio Grande." Senior thesis, Princeton University, 1999.

Inglis, Jack M. *A History of Vegetation on the Rio Grande Plain.* Texas Parks and Wildlife Department Bulletin No. 45. Austin, Texas, 1964.

Jelks, Edward B. "The Founding Meeting of the Society for Historical Archaeology, 6 January 1967." *Journal of the Society for Historical Archaeology* 27, no. 1 (1993): 10–11.

"Journalistic Overview of Refugees in Their Own Land." n.d. A collection of news articles from many different newspapers. A copy is available at the Zapata County Historical Commission, Zapata, Tex.

Krieger, Alex D., and Jack T. Hughes. *Archaeological Salvage in the Falcón Reservoir Area, Progress Report No. 1.* Report to the National Park Service, 1950. On file at the Texas Archaeological Research Laboratory (TARL), Balcones Research Center, University of Texas at Austin.*

Leggett, Mike. "Draining Life from the Rio Grande." *Austin American-Statesman,* June 15, 2001, A1–10.

Lott, Virgil N., and Virginia M. Fenwick. *People and Plots on the Rio Grande.* San Antonio: Naylor, 1957.*

Lott, Virgil N., and Mercurio Martinez. *The Kingdom of Zapata.* San Antonio: Naylor, 1953.*

McVey, Lori Brown. *Guerrero Viejo: A Photographic Essay.* Laredo, Tex.: Nuevo Santander Museum Complex, Department of Education, 1988.

Montejano, David. *Anglos and Mexicans in the Making of Texas, 1836–1987.* Austin: University of Texas Press, 1987.

Mumford, Lewis. *Sticks and Stones: A Study of American Architecture and Civilization.* New York: Harcourt, Brace, and World, 1955.*

Myrthe, A. T. [pseud.] *Ambrosio de Letinez; or, the First Texian Novel.* 2 vols. Facsimile reproduction of 1842 ed. Austin: Steck, 1967.*

National Register of Historic Places for Texas. Files of the Texas Historical Commission Library. Austin, Tex.

*The New Handbook of Texas.* Austin: Texas State Historical Association, 1996. Information may also be accessed online at www.tsha.utexas.edu/handbook/online/.

Olmsted, Frederick Law. *A Journey through Texas.* New York: Dix, Edwards, 1857.*

*Our Catholic Heritage in Texas, 1519–1936.* Prepared under the Auspices of the Knights of Columbus of Texas. By Carlos E. Castañeda. Vol. 3. Austin, Tex.: Von Boeckmann-Jones, 1936.*

Pertula, Tim. "The Falcon Sites: Present and Past Destruction." Texas beyond History. www.texasbeyondhistory.net/falcon/destruction.html.

Pierce, Frank C. *A Brief History of the Lower Rio Grande Valley.* Menasha, Wisc.: George Banta Publishing, 1917.*

Poniatowska, Elena. *Guerrero Viejo.* Photography by Richard Payne. Houston: Anchorage Press, 1998.

Ramírez, Emilia Schunior. *Ranch Life in Hidalgo County after 1850.* Edinburg, Tex.: New Santander Press, 1971.

Ramsey, Closner. "Scrapbook of the Lower Rio Grande Valley." In the author's possession. *

*Regional Assessment of Water Quality in the Rio Grande Basin.* Records, Texas Natural Resource Conservation Commission. Archives and Information Services Division, Texas State Library and Archives Commission.

Rudofsky, Bernard. *Architecture without Architects.* New York: Museum of Modern Art, distributed by Doubleday, 1964.

Scott, Florence Johnson. *Historical Heritage of the Lower Rio Grande.* 1937; Waco, Tex.: Texian Press, 1966.*

*A Shared Experience.* Ed. Mario L. Sánchez. 2nd ed. Austin: Los Caminos del Rio Heritage Project and the Texas Historical Commission, 1994.

Simons, Helen, and Cathryn A. Hoyt, eds. *A Guide to Hispanic Texas.* Austin: University of Texas Press, 1996.

Stanislawski, Dan. "Early Spanish Town Planning." *Geographical Review* 38 (1947).*

Tijerina, Andrés. *Tejanos and Texas under the Mexican Flag, 1831–1836.* College Station: Texas A&M University Press, 1994.

Vigness, David M. "The Lower Rio Grande Valley, 1836–1846." Master's thesis, University of Texas at Austin, 1948.*

Vines, Robert A. *Trees, Shrubs, and Woody Vines of the Southwest.* Austin: University of Texas Press, 1960.*

Weiner, Tim. "Water Crisis Grows into a Test of U.S.-Mexico Relations." *New York Times,* May 24, 2002, A3.

# Index

ISBN-13: 978-1-60344-011-0
ISBN-10: 1-60344-011-9